smart sex stuff for kids ™

SMART SEX STUFF

FOR KIDS 7-17

PRACTICAL INFORMATION & IDEAS
FOR KIDS, PARENTS & TEACHERS

By
Carole Marsh

GALLOPADE
INTERNATIONAL

3

smart sex stuff for kids ™

Coweta Public Library System
85 Literary Lane
Newnan, GA 30265
770-683-2052

Copyright ©2008 Carole Marsh/Gallopade International

Managing Editor: Sherry Moss
Senior Editor: Janice Baker
Content Design: Melissa Kotch
Cover Design: The Publishing Designers | The OGRAPHIS team

Gallopade is proud to be a member and supporter of these educational organizations and associations:

American Booksellers Association
American Library Association
International Reading Association
National Association for Gifted Children
The National School Supply and Equipment Association
The National Council for the Social Studies
Museum Store Association
Association of Partners for Public Lands

REVIEWERS GIVE SMART SEX STUFF BOOKS AN A⁺!

In this excellent resource, Marsh covers a lot of basic sexual information but does not skirt the issue of AIDS and other sexually transmitted diseases. This common-sensical, and sometimes humorous, approach stresses choices based on information and maturity. It is geared for children as young as seven, with parental guidance. Young teens can read it on their own. Recommended for all public libraries.
—Susan McBride/ Library Journal

Addresses all the questions and misconceptions children have in plain language, interspersed with humor. Includes information about AIDS.
—Planned Parenthood LINKLINE

Finally, for young people and their parents—a book on sex, simply written for today's school children—about their body changes and how to learn about sex the safe way.
—Josephine Hookway, R.N., OB-GYN, N.P.

A RICH RESOURCE—a must for parents! Clearly stated, sensible, and an effective combination of humor and seriousness. Kids can be sex smart.
—L. Chennault, Teacher of the Year

5

Out of the ever-increasing titles competing for attention in this area—these merit a well-deserved consideration and enthusiastic recommendation based on general excellence; valuable additions to personal, community or academic library sex ed inventories.
—Jim Cox, Midwest Book Review

Clarity of thought and presentation, inherently interesting material, and a flair for the written word makes Smart Sex Stuff™ for Kids 7-17 & Their Parents & Teachers a MUST acquisition for parents, teachers, libraries, paraprofessionals, as well as the kids themselves.
—Diane Donovan, Book Reviewer, San Francisco, CA

If you have a child or student who refuses to read anything that looks like a textbook, this might get their attention. Adolescents not ready to engage in sexual intimacy will find lots of support.
—Ann Barrett, Education Outreach Coordinator, Planned Parenthood Toronto
(in the SIECCAN Newsletter)

6

SMART SEX STUFF FOR KIDS™

OTHER BOOKS BY CAROLE MARSH

SMART SEX STUFF FOR KIDS 7-17;
PRACTICAL INFORMATION & IDEAS FOR KIDS, PARENTS & TEACHERS

A PERIOD IS MORE THAN A PUNCTUATION MARK!
SMART SEX STUFF FOR GIRLS

SPERM, SQUIRM & OTHER SQUIGGLY STUFF!
SMART SEX STUFF FOR BOYS

7

TABLE OF CONTENTS
Smart Sex Stuff for Kids 7-17

©Car... ...llopade International/8o... -536-2GET/www.gallopade.com/Smart Sex Stuff for Kids 7-17

TABLE OF CONTENTS
(Continued)

What do you call parents who only teach their teenagers abstinence?

GRANDPARENTS!

Dear Kid,

If you are reading this book—it is dedicated to you.

Flip through the pages to see the couple kiss!

Sex is like algebra or cars or history or life—there are endless things to learn. You're never too young to get started...and you're never too old or experienced to learn something new—especially when there's always something new to learn. Yes, even about sex!

Sex can be **silly** and **SERIOUS**.

It can be complicated and confusing, or simple and straight-forward. It can be good. And bad.

It can be **A-mazing** or **Zzz** (boring—really!)

Some sex stuff will apply to you, and some won't—but you need to know about it all.

I hope this book gives you lots of answers to your questions about all sorts of "sex stuff."

Carole Marsh
Former kid

Dear Parents & Teachers Around the World,

More than 20 years ago, as the new subject of AIDS continued to dominate world headlines, and each subsequent article and revelation edged downward in age until it was clear our children were going to be affected—I knew I had to write a book on sex for kids. For young kids. (I don't know about you, but to talk about sex and death and the specifics that explain the connection to children 7, 8 and 9 seemed awfully young to me, but essential. I cringed, but pressed on.)

I believe that at an early age, children should begin to learn about the lifetime of sexuality ahead of them. Even if every child lived up to the ideal: "No sex until marriage"—that wouldn't let us off the hook to explain all aspects of sexuality—their own...and others.

This was vividly brought to my clear attention *more than 20 years ago* by a fourth grade teacher at our local elementary school. "You must do a book on sex education!" she insisted. When I asked why, she responded, "We have three fourth graders in our county school system who are pregnant." [This means they were ages 9 or 10, folks.] I was astounded. Frankly I had never heard of such a thing. "The book or books you write need to be usable by kids that young. Girls are getting their periods earlier and earlier, and becoming sexually active at a younger and younger age. Also, I need the information! Girls ask me questions and I have few answers. Help us, *please*."

I insisted that in spite of the fact that I had been writing for children all my career, I knew nothing about sex education. [I had given my own kids a "book" to read; obviously a book that would be very outdated at this point.] But when I looked in my files, I discovered a wealth of collected research on all kinds of sex subjects. Like what? Like responsibility, self-esteem, reproduction, the basic birds and bees, unusual and humorous sex antics in nature, and many other things. I was flabbergasted and fascinated. I realized that, unwittingly, I had been preparing to help children in this sensitive and crucial area for many years. I began to write!

12

Of course we hope our children never encounter sexual abuse, date rape. Do not have to drop out of school because of pregnancy. Avoid risk of sexually transmitted diseases. But when we do not give them a larger picture to measure a small concern or crisis by, we rob them of the ability to achieve a more secure, stable, workable perspective in which to consider even simple, scheduled items as they appear on their personal sexual agenda.

In writing this book, I have tried to be every parent, every nationality, every religion. And while I cannot possibly have satisfied everyone, please know I sincerely tried to put myself in your caring, compassionate, concerned position.

Do not embrace the book wholeheartedly. Question it and encourage your children to do the same. This questioning and assessing and deciding is what the book is all about! But, do not dismiss it in its entirety because you disagree with a word, a sentence, a section. Tear out a page if you must!—but don't deny your children access to this valid and valuable information.

Even if there were no such thing as AIDS, STDs, Internet predators, etc., we must present our children with a program of sex education so that they can prepare responsibly for the decisions that are theirs to make—no matter how we might wish we could make them for them.

I truly trust kids to listen. They may laugh. And many will disagree and disobey. But I believe our efforts will impact their sexual activities and attitudes.

Just because it is too late for some and we will never convince others—the pendulum that can swing so widely from Victorian modesty skirts on piano legs to proliferate promiscuity can swing again. If we can help the ebb and flow of peer pressure eddy in time to catch the next generation of children in a pool of positive response to the idea of abstinence until monogamy, or safe sex everytime—we will have done a great thing!

How should you use the book? Only you know. There are some kids who probably need to be locked in a room until they read it and pass a test! Most kids

would welcome their own personal copy. If they know you have read it, perhaps they'll feel freer to ask questions or be more open to discussion.

You can control the information your child receives by using the book as a joint reference. If you both know you have a source to go to (and you start young), how much easier those questions—and answers—will be!

Forever for Kids,

Carole Marsh

P.S. The plot thickens. After my Smart Sex Stuff for Kids™ series came out, I was invited to speak to a large gathering of Planned Parenthood leaders. I quaked in my boots! I was just a writer, not a bona fide sex educator. However, my talk was extremely well-received and appreciated. But then, the audience grew oddly quiet. You could have heard a pin drop. I feared I had said or done something wrong. A hand went up on the front row. When I recognized the attractive, businesslike woman, she confessed, "We have some questions. We have some situations in our district that we do not know how to address." "Ok," I answered nervously. The woman then told me that she had two incidences of older (age 9) brothers molesting (meaning intercourse) their younger sisters. What an aberration I thought to myself, knowing I had no clue what to do or say about such a thing. Heads began to nod in the audience and more hands went up as more districts admitted, "Us, too. And we don't know what to do."

On a lighter note (which may make us all feel better), many of these professional sex educators said that while they were great at counseling others, they were completely uncomfortable (as in mortified!) to tackle the "talk" with their own children. I went to educate and got educated!

Fast-forward 20 years and we find:

•The teen pregnancy rate is on the increase
•The media is blaring more frequent and blatant sexual messages and images

14

•There was no Internet 20 years ago, and now...
•Abstinence-only is a great theory (and practice) for some; but the fact is that depriving (for that is what it is) kids of knowledge of contraceptives puts them at risk for pregnancy and/or disease *unnecessarily*.
•And news headlines include teachers molesting students, children molesting children, and much more—more than we can, should, or want to ignore responding to.

But the thing I really want you to know is this: Smart Sex Stuff for Kids™ (the entire program) was bought and used by groups as conservative as Southern Baptist church libraries...and as aggressive as NFL-supported boys' homes. (Just imagine me on the phone with former Washington Redskins coach Joe Gibbs "talking sex!" From women who said, "Having this book when I was a girl would have changed my life" to the friends of my children who came to read the drafts of the books at my house (because their parents "wouldn't talk to them"...and many more positive experiences only showed me the dire need in this area.

In many countries, sex education is open, thorough, and effective. In America, we have our problems with this sensitive issue, don't we? But you know, if we are open and brave and err (if you will) on the side of full-disclosure, fascinating facts, early education, and a sense of humor—we can save many, many children from so much grief. How, indeed, can we expect them to be responsible if we don't shoulder our responsibility in this area.

Actually, it's not as hard as you think. I've learned to love "sex stuff" and find it a joy to help kids learn about their bodies, their opportunities, their responsibilities, and their futures. Please give this book, this series a shot and a fair chance. I promise you'll be laughing in just few pages and "get" what I am preaching.

Sex education for boys and girls at the age they really need it (and that's not age 17 folks!) is no longer an option—it's essential.

15

Dino Love

According to the National Academy of Sciences, adolescent pregnancy isn't a new thing. Dinosaurs had teen (and even pre-teen) births. Dinosaurs apparently went through dino puberty as early as age 8. Most dinosaurs went on to live until about age 30, although some could live to age 60. The scientific research does not indicate whether dino parents were upset over these adolescent pregnancies, who raised the kids, or if dino child support was involved. At least there were no diapers involved.

SMART SEX STUFF

FOR KIDS 7-17

PRACTICAL INFORMATION & IDEAS
FOR KIDS, PARENTS & TEACHERS

Texas Sexes

In 2008, the state of Texas passed a law mandating high schools provide "parenting advice" to all students. A new curriculum teaches parenting and "paternity awareness." One goal of the new required studies is to crack down on fathers who fail to support their children. Presumably, this "preventive role" will help. Perhaps it would help even more if the curriculum was adapted for junior high...and possibly younger. You can never instill the concept of sexual maturity and responsibility early enough or often enough.

STRAIGHT STUFF

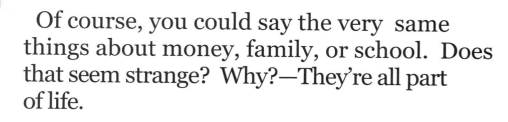

STRAIGHT STUFF

Sex Is A Fact of Life

Sex is a fact of *everyone's* life. This is a book of sex facts. Some silly. Some strange. Some serious. Some, *very* serious.

You have a lifetime of sex.

Sometimes, that means very little— you aren't concerned with sex at all. Other times, *sex is the main thing on your mind!*

Sometimes you're concerned with your own body; other times, with the bodies of others.

Sometimes your sex questions are urgent; your problems major. But most times, your sexuality is just a regular, normal, ordinary part of your everyday life and no real big deal.

Sometimes, sex seems like the greatest thing since peanut butter. Other days, *"Who needs it?!"*

Of course, you could say the very same things about money, family, or school. Does that seem strange? Why?—They're all part of life.

And so is sex.

20

Your Sex Life Is Your Own

Your body belongs to you. You'll have it all your life.

It's yours to take care of, keep to yourself, or share. So, *your* feelings, *your* opinions, *your* needs, *your* ideas matter most.

But, maybe you're confused about what you want, need, think, what's right, wrong, good, bad, true, false, smart, stupid, silly, weird. There are 3 ways to help that:

💜 *BE INFORMED:* Reading this book is a good start!

💜 *BE SMART:* The more you know, think through, plan ahead—the better things work out.

💜 *BE IN CONTROL* = *being mature.* Becoming mature about your sexuality takes time, patience, education, and a lot of trust and faith in the people who care most about you—*your parents.*

You are responsible for your sex life—**all** your life.

You have to take responsibility for when you become involved sexually with another person. *You* must take responsibility for when, and if, you have children.

21

Sex is a good thing, there's no doubt. But like any good thing, it has to be responsibly handled. (*Or*, it can turn into a big headache—or worse—pretty fast!)

Have a sense of sexual humor. Sex is a *fun* subject! It's interesting—often, just plain amazing. It involves our bodies... and our brains. It has a history. In fact, geography, math, science, and most everything else, relate to sex.

These days, we're all quite aware that some things about sex can be pretty bad. The sex-related disease called AIDS is about the baddest thing we know about sex these days.

It's not my goal in this book to "preach" to you. Not to "fuss." Not "boss." In fact, a lot of adults would probably be "all over my case" if I tried to tell you what's right or wrong about sex.

Why? Because, as you probably already know, people have very different opinions about sex matters. And they usually feel pretty strongly about those opinions.

You will have strong opinions about sex. Hopefully, after you read this book, your opinions will be based on **facts**, so you can be smart and responsible about sex.

22

There will always be more to learn about sex, but the facts are a good place to start. Some you may know. Some may be new. Some may be different from "facts" you've heard.

Frankly, I think you're already a pretty smart kid to try to get some information on sex from an adult and a book, instead of just from your friends (who can be **real** wrong!) or television and the Internet (which can be **real** dumb!!)

So, let's get to some SEX STUFF!

23

"Well, kid, it's about time we had a talk about sex."

"Sure—what did you want to know?"

What Do You Know?

What do you know about sex already? Well, if you're 7, not very much at all—which is fine. If you're 17, you probably already know a lot. Maybe more about some things...less about others. *Maybe* you don't know as much as you think you do. And maybe you know more than you should! And, maybe some of what you know isn't even right.

For example, do you think the following are true?

1. A baby pops out of its mother's belly button.

2. You can't get pregnant if you wear high heels while having sexual intercourse.

24

3. If a boy does not like girls, he's gay.

All of the above all *not* true. But counselors at youth clinics have met many kids 7-17 who believe they are. A personnel manager at a fast food chain says that when many students fill out employment applications they mark the blank beside SEX: *"Yes"*, *"No"*, *"Twice a week"*, etc.—instead of just *MALE* or *FEMALE*!

Sometimes adults shake their heads in disbelief at things kids believe about sex. But really, sex is no different from a recipe, physics, or your bank statement—while you're learning to cook or phyzz or balance, it's easy to get confused or mixed-up.

No one needs to feel bad about being ignorant about sexual matters. The most important thing is to get the facts and get them straight.

Why don't you know more about sex? Well, frankly, it's not your fault. Many parents are reluctant to talk to their kids about sex.

Your parents or teachers may cover the basics, but never get to "tough stuff," such as contraception, abortion, and sex diseases.

25

So, why—what seems like all of a sudden—are most adults eager for kids to learn more about sex, and at a younger age?

1. Kids are involved with sex at a younger age. By age 19, 8 out of 10 boys and 7 out of 10 girls in the United States have had sexual intercourse. Two out of three say they don't use any regular birth control. Perhaps even more shocking, before age 13, 9% of boys and 4% of girls become sexually active.

(It might surprise you that many teens are deciding to wait to have sex. Like they did with smoking and drinking and drugs—a lot of smart kids have decided that the hassle and worry over getting caught, pregnant, AIDS or another disease—just isn't worth it. Since a LOT of kids are changing their minds, peer pressure is also easing up—which will only make it easier for you to say, "Not yet" to sex!)

2. AIDS. There have been sex diseases for as long as there's been sex. But never one that killed so many people. Because this deadly disease can only be prevented by **not** having sex—adults have decided they must be sure every person, every age, understands this.

26

3. The third reason is very important. Let me give you an example:

Mothers, whose kids had a baby, were interviewed. They were asked what they'd have done differently to discourage their kids from becoming involved in sex...and what they might have done or said to be sure they would have at least taken precautions against disease and pregnancy. What do you think the mothers said?

NOTHING.

The Moms all agreed: AFTER THEY HAD SAID AND DONE ALL THEY COULD ABOUT SEX—WHAT THEIR KIDS DID WAS UP TO THEM, AND OUT OF THE PARENTS' CONTROL.

WELL! Needless to say, no parent likes to admit that. But we all know this to be one of the truest facts of life: that only up to a certain point can parents help, inform, advise about sex. The rest is up to you. **You** are responsible for your lifetime of sex.

SO, LET'S LEARN SOMETHING ABOUT IT!

TALK ABOUT IT?!

A poll asked:
"Do you & your parents discuss sex?"
49% of parents said "Yes"
But only 23% of their kids agreed!

A⁺ For Attitude!

Perhaps you're reading this book yourself, or, an adult is reading it to or with you. You may be a parent or teacher looking for information and ideas for handling sex education with children. You all have one thing in common—you aren't going to agree on everything about sex.

We humans are so preoccupied with our own sexuality, we forget sex is very common and ordinary. For all our worries about sex, it must work pretty well— look at all the creatures on Earth!

28

You'll form opinions and make decisions, not only about your own sex life, but about the sex lives of others. Put yourself in the other person's place. Not agreeing does not have to be the same as not understanding.

This is why sex education is so important and a never-ending study. As we learn more about the human body and mind, we must update our information and ideas about sex.

So, kids, give adults the benefit of the doubt. Ask questions. Keep an open mind. Adults: likewise! How will kids know unless they ask? It may seem they're too young to know some things. But if they've heard a word or term, what good is it for them to be ignorant of its meaning?

Have a good attitude toward sex, sex education, and people's varying opinions, values, and beliefs.

Myth & Mythtakes

One reason it's easy to feel confused about sex is that sex is always changing. That would not seem like it would be true, but it is! Think about these changes:

• Victorian ladies put "modesty" skirts on their legs—their PIANO legs!

• It wasn't until the Stone Age when people decided that maybe they should get married before having sex— and only have sex with the person they were married to.

• For thousands of years, masturbation was a "no-no." Now it's seen as a normal, healthy part of sexuality.

• Just when we thought we knew all about most sex-related diseases, here came AIDS. It was only a few years ago that this new disease appeared, causing us to have to stop and learn a lot more about sex and its consequences.

• While parents have always said they wanted kids to learn about sex in the home, current studies show kids are doing just that—by having sex at home after school, while their parents are still at work. (Do *you* think that's what parents had in mind?!)

30

• Someone invents *"outercourse"*, which means doing everything except having *"intercourse."* (Of course!)

• You can make a deposit in a "Cryobank." No, not of money, or tears, but of sperm, which is frozen until you want to use it to produce a baby. (Come to think of it, CRYobank is not a bad name for it, is it?)

The things that are TRUE about sex can be more surprising than anything you'll ever make up! Let's take a look at just a sampling of how wide a variety of sex exists:

• Sex between a male and a female isn't even necessary for reproduction in most species! *(Aren't we glad that doesn't include us!)*

• Trichonymphas - live in the intestines of termites and cockroaches and turn into a male or female. The small male enters the larger female completely! Sometimes a male gets mixed up and climbs into another male. *("Oops! Excuse me!!")*

• Consider the sex life of an oyster. They spend all their time in "beds," but can't get together with the opposite sex because they are anchored in place. *(Talk about being "stuck" without a date!)*

31

• In the fall, the Samoan palolo worm becomes a sex machine and has the sea frothing in an orgy just before dawn on the first day of the last quarter of the October and November moons! *(Mark your calendar!)*

• Grunion "run" out of the water, up on the sand, swirl and writhe and go back into the sea sexually satisfied—all in about 25 seconds!

• Scientists say if creatures live in large groups (mostly female), it's better to be a male, and vice versa. *(But, I think we could have figured that out for ourselves, don't you?)*

• The male wrasse fish has a harem of several females. If he dies, the largest, oldest female takes his place by becoming a male!

• The male seahorse has the babies in that family!

• A scorpion fly is long and thin. It's so lazy, it finds it easier to get sex and food by pretending to be a female and attracting a male!

• The ruffled grouse "drums" up a sex partner by making a drumming noise. It's hard to tell girl drumming from boy drumming. If a male "drums" and another grouse shows up and punches him—he knows it's another male. If a grouse shows up and ignores him—it's a female. Sometimes they mistake the sound of a farm tractor for drumming and get friendly with the machine!

• Earthworms, or night crawlers, each have a male and a female sex organ—which fertilize each other!

• Sea cucumbers and sea hares form a long chain and reproduce, as many as 12 at a time—each one gives sperm to the next!

• When helix snails meet, they press a part of their foot against one another and feel each other all over with tentacles and lips. They each have a penis which they put into the other to exchange sperm.

• Consider the sex life of a slug *(ugh?!)* They hang from a tree branch and mate in mid-air, twist together and insert club-shaped penises into each other. When they are done, they fall to the ground. *(I would, too, wouldn't you?!)*

• Aphids or plant lice produce live young which live inside the parent. These live young can produce live young which live inside them while they live inside, etc. *(Saves rent?)*

• Whiptail lizards are female and hatch only females! *Huh?*

• Giant Japanese male spider crabs have twin penises shaped like corkscrews!

33

• The sex life of a Chinese bamboo plant occurs only once around the world—every 120 years!

• In their dark sea home, anglerfish have a hard time finding one another. The female is large, the male tiny. When they do get together, the male becomes a parasite on the female. Since she gives him both food and sex, he can never let her go. *(I saw a soap opera like this once!)*

• Fireflies or lightning bugs are actually flirting with their lights!

• It's no wonder the male praying mantis prays—the female eats him alive from the head down during sex.

• The male toad must cling to the female toad's back for 3-26 days to mate. Sometimes the male is so eager to have sex that he climbs onto the back of a rock by mistake!

RECIPE FOR A BABY

INGREDIENTS: 1 Egg/1 Sperm
UTENSILS: 1 Penis/1 Vagina

TO PREPARE: Take 1 erect penis and place in 1 vagina. Ejaculate. One sperm will fertilize one egg. (Discard other 399,999 sperm.) Let fertilized egg bake in warm uterus for nine months. When baby is done, it will eject from the vagina. Wrap in blanket to keep warm.

Serves: 2 for 18 years/**Cost per serving:** @$100,000+

How 'Bout Us Humans?

The most important human sex organ is the brain! Human sexuality is just as varied as that we have just seen in the animal and insect world:

• If you mature into a person who prefers to have sex with someone of the opposite sex, you are a *heterosexual.*

• As some people mature, they realize they are sexually attracted to members of their own sex. They are *homosexuals*. (I'm not talking about a girl having a crush on a female teacher, or a boy who masturbates with the guys. Many boys and girls try out at least one sex activity with someone of their own sex. This doesn't mean they're "gay"—it's just another part of the early exploration of your sexuality.)

A *homosexual* is a man who knows he definitely prefers to have sex only with another man. Homosexual men have sex either orally (one puts his penis in the other's mouth) or anally (putting the penis in the anus.)

A *lesbian* is a woman who has sex only with another woman. Homosexual women have sex orally by putting the mouth to the genitals, or by putting their fingers into the other's vagina.

• Some people have sex with people of the same **and** of the opposite sex—they are *bisexual*.

• Sometimes, a person discovers they are *transsexual*. (This is different from *transvestites* or people who like to dress in clothes of the sex they are not.) Even though their body may have male or female sex organs, in their brain, they know they are really the opposite sex. Sometimes, they have surgery to alter their sex organs.

• Some people have sex in exchange for money. They are *prostitutes*. Prostitutes can be male or female. In most countries, prostitution is illegal. Kids who run away from home and kids on drugs often turn to prostitution. As we'll learn in this book, having sex with a lot of different partners can be very hazardous to your health.

• *Kinky* sex is what we call the unique sex activities that about 10% of adults are involved in. Usually these people associate sexual pleasure with pain, probably as a result of some experience in their past. Some of these activities can be simple and harmless. Other activities can be like a sexual game, where one partner pretends to be the master of another. While it may sound sort of silly, sometimes, *sado-masochists* (people who get sexual pleasure from being hurt or hurting another) can do just that—hurt each other!

• An *orgy* is a whole group of people having sex together.

• *"Ear" sex* = sex over the telephone. There are numbers you can call where a person will talk sexy to you. Some people masturbate while they listen. These calls cost money and are usually charged to your phone bill or credit card.

37

• Some people use *vibrators*, which are small devices held against the genitals to make you have an orgasm. You might have felt the same sensation on a bouncing school bus.

• *Adultery* is when a husband or wife has sex with someone other than their own husband or wife.

Your sexual preference is a part of you—the way you are and were meant to be. If a heterosexual and a homosexual made a list of all the ways they are alike (including *"want to be loved, want to have a home, like ice cream"*), they would find a very long list. If they list the ways they are different, *"Like other guys"/"Prefer girls"*—might be the only thing on that list!

That one person's lifetime of sex includes being *celibate* (not having sex), and another's means marrying someone of the opposite sex, and a third's includes caring for and having sex with someone of the same sex—does not make one more right, one less happy, one better, one worse, etc.

If sex is always changing, what in the world can the future hold?

• Biologists see no reason why an embryo fertilized in a lab cannot be implanted in a man's abdomen, which would later be delivered by a Cesarean Section. (If you think I'm trying to say a man could have a baby—that's right. But there haven't been any volunteers yet!)

38

• And then there's sex in weightless space... and what new will aliens add to our knowledge of sex, if they should finally show their face—and everything else?!

Even now there are penis implants so that a man who could not have an erection—can, and therefore, happily continue his sex life. Will bionic genitals be next?

The point is: There's always something new under the sexual sun! And that sun shines everywhere!

As people travel, live and work around the world and in space, they take their culture, language, ideas—and sexuality with them.

The one thing that is universal is that everyone truly wants what is best for their children—in education, in lifestyle, and in sex, whether those kids are 7, 17 or 71!

39

Coloring the Dangers of Sex?

The Roman Catholic Church in New York has spearheaded a campaign of coloring books that warn children about sex crimes. A guardian angel guides the youngsters through the maze of do's and don't's. The coloring books cover not keeping secrets from your parents, who to allow to touch you, and Internet chat rooms.

GIRL STUFF & BOY STUFF

GIRL STUFF & BOY STUFF

You're lucky. Today we know a lot about the body and how it works. Everyone's more open about sex. And why not? There's nothing bad or ugly or secret about our body and its functions.

Since there are very few things in life that belong to you 100%—this makes your body very special and valuable.

You'll have this body all your life, so you might as well learn about it. Since everybody has a body and everybody's body pretty much works the same way, we probably all spend too much time worrying if ours is good enough, big enough, or doing what it's supposed to. Once you understand your body, you can put that energy somewhere else. *(In your math homework?!)*

Girls—Let's Get Physical!

One day, when you're around 9 or 10, the pituitary gland at the base of your brain says, "Yikes! It's time for this girl to grow up!"

42

So it sends word to your body and slowly but surely, it yawns and stretches and gets down to the business of transforming a girl into a woman.

One of the first things you notice is your breasts begin to pooch out. Since no one can see your bossy pituitary, but you think everyone can see the new little bulges under your tee shirt, you immediately get self-conscious.

Is this supposed to happen? Now? How do I know? Who can I ask? How do I know if they are telling the truth? What in the world is going on? Help!

What can you do about these changes? Not much! Everyone is subject to the schedule for their own, individual body, and must trust that things are proceeding according to plan.

Not everyone's thrilled about growing up. *Being a kid isn't so bad!* But, it's part of your lifetime of sex, so accept and enjoy it.

For a girl, maturing sexually includes the following. (While some may happen sooner or later, faster or slower, in sudden spurts or slowpokey, they eventually all happen in pretty much this order of events:)

1. The endocrine glands (pituitary, thyroid, parathyroids and adrenals) send out chemicals called hormones into that

highway in your body: Bloodstream One! This has been happening since you were born *(didn't hurt a bit, did it?!)*, but now the hormones speed around faster and faster. Here's what the extra hormone activity causes:

2. The dark circles around your nipples puff up. Next, the entire breast grows. One may grow faster than the other. They may ache. White, milky stuff may leak out. But it's all just part of the growing caused by those busy hormones.

It takes about 3 years for your breasts to do their growing up, so don't waste time being impatient or trying to help them along. *(Those "magic" creams don't work anyway.)*

While growing girls worry if their breasts are too

big or small,

most women are very happy with the final results.

Some women with large breasts prefer smaller ones, and even have a very safe operation to reduce them. Women with smaller breasts often discover they can wear many attractive clothing designs not suitable for large-breasted women. Some do have surgery to make their breasts larger, but such an operation can have complications.

In some countries, men and women consider other parts of the body to be more sexually attractive than the breasts. In

44

some cultures, small breasts are preferred to large ones. Also, fads about breast size come and go. We get so focused on the size of breasts, we forget they are primarily there to produce milk for a newborn baby.

The female breast is a beautiful thing. If they weren't such an "up front" part of your body, they probably wouldn't receive all this attention. *(I mean, when's the last time you checked the size of the back of your knees?)* So, get your Mom or a friend or a store clerk to help you pick out a pretty bra and enjoy your new-grown beauty!

3. Hair begins to grow under your arms. The hair on your legs may get darker and stiffer. And hair begins to grow in the pubic area. In some countries, it's common for women to let this hair grow naturally. In others, women usually shave their underarm and leg hair. I'm sure you and your Mom can agree when the best time to start this practice will be. *(C'mon, Mom—remember when **you** were a girl!)*

Some girls may feel they're "growing a moustache," but this is just a little additional hair over your upper lip. If you have light hair, you may never notice it. If you have darker hair, it's easier to see. If it makes you uncomfortable or embarrassed, it can be simply *(but carefully!)* shaved off, or a dermatologist (skin doctor) can explain other remedies.

In fact, it's only because others can see (or you *think* they've noticed) that you pay so much attention to these outward changes. But really and truly, far more important things are happening!

4. Your reproductive organs, which are what make you able to have a baby, are also growing and changing.

 The ovaries hold the eggs needed to create a baby. They begin to produce female hormones. These estrogens cause the reproductive organs to grow: the ovaries; the Fallopian tubes (that the eggs travel through to...); the uterus (where an egg may grow into a baby) and the vagina, which is the opening between your legs that leads to these reproductive organs.

5. Outside your vagina, the external genitals also change. In addition to hair growth, the vulva, which is the folds of skin and flesh around the opening of the vagina begins to mature.

(Just so we can get this straight: Yep, a girl has 3 outside openings between her legs:

• The urethra, which she urinates from.
• The anal opening, which her bowels move from.
• The vagina, which is used during sexual intercourse and is also the path a baby takes out of the mother's body when it's being born. This is also the opening she has her period from.

No, things don't all get mixed up or confused just because they are close together. I mean your eye and nose are real close, but you don't "blow" your eye when you have a cold—even though you might "look down your nose" at someone?!)

46

Within the folds of the vulva, where the lips of flesh come to a point in the upper part of the pubic area, is the clitoris. This is a small, sensitive bump that feels so good when you have an orgasm.

What's an orgasm? A very good and special feeling in your genitals that comes at the heighth of your sexual excitement. For a boy, this is when you ejaculate. For a girl, it's a throbbing shiver in the area of the clitoris or vagina. It lasts a short time, then you feel very relaxed. It's one of the things people enjoy most about sex. It feels good and it's nice to help your partner have this good feeling. You don't have to have sex with someone to have an orgasm. You may have one just thinking about sex, or while masturbating, or when you have sexual contact (but not necessarily intercourse) with another person.

6. Your appetite increases because you are growing taller and your arms and legs and hips and the rest of your body must also grow and fill out. This is good. *(You'd look pretty silly with a woman's body and little girl legs, wouldn't you?)*

Some girls get so concerned about their weight they never feel they're thin enough, no matter how slim they are. This fear of being fat causes them to do some drastic things—like starve themselves. Or, they may "pig out", then make themselves throw the food back up. The words for these problems are *anorexia* and *bulimia*. If they sound like bad problems—well, they are. They can even kill you.

47

So, remember, that although everyone wants to be physically attractive and knows that being fat's not healthy, nothing's more important than good nutrition. There are times—especially when your body is growing rapidly—that you need extra calories *(now, I didn't say run out and eat 3 chocolate sundaes and 4 pizzas!)*

7. All these changes are reflected in your mental attitude. You may begin to think more about grown up things, including your body and all that's happening to it. These physical changes are not only physical—they're emotional. And one of the physical things girls get most emotional about is their PERIOD!

A (Period) Is More Than A Punctuation Mark!

Once upon a time, the menstrual cycle was treated like a mystery. Now, it's something everyone knows about—even boys, thanks to sex education.

And, once, no one may have explained to a young girl what to expect the first time. As you can imagine, it might come as a big surprise. You're lucky to be able to get some honest, accurate and timely information.

Having your first period is evidence you're becoming a woman and your body's preparing to be able to have a child, when and if that time ever comes. Since that's how we all get here in the first place, and that's what keeps life on earth "keeping on"—it's no wonder that everyone in most every country and culture considers this first period a big deal!

(Of course, no one usually gives you a new car or anything great like that, but don't be surprised to be "Congratulated!")

What Is A Period? Well, first let's talk about what is isn't. It isn't a "curse" or anything awful or terrible. It isn't something to be ashamed of or embarrassed about. It isn't something somebody knows you're having by looking at you. You're not sick. It's not dirty.

49

How did periods get such a bad reputation? Easy: lack of information; old-fashioned ideas; and a long history of "old wive's tales" created a lot of silly superstitions, even though for a long time we've known they aren't true.

A period is really just one part of your reproductive cycle—a very ordinary and normal event that takes place over and over. The entire menstrual cycle is the repeated preparation of a woman's body to reproduce another human being *(a little one, called a baby, of course)*—and here's how the cycle goes:

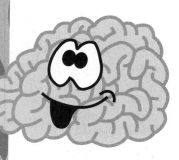

Back to the brain! The pituitary gland shoots out hormones that travel Bloodstream Highway One to the ovaries. The hormones cause one of the ovaries to begin ripening an egg. Don't worry, this egg's not as big as a chicken egg or anything—it's almost invisible!

Where do these eggs come from? When a girl is born, her ovaries contain about 400,000 eggs. Only about 400 of these will ever be released from the ovaries. We really aren't sure why you have so many "spares."

Usually an egg is ripened in one ovary one month and the other ovary (you have two), the next. After an egg has ripened, it comes out of the ovary. This is called ovulation. Most girls never feel this happen.

This menstrual or reproductive cycle takes about 28 days altogether. Ovulation occurs about halfway through the cycle, or about 14 days after each period, once you begin to have them.

The egg goes into the Fallopian tube nearest it and travels down to the uterus. Even in this tube, the egg can be fertilized.

How does an egg get fertilized? Through sexual intercourse, when a man puts his penis into a woman's vagina. Sperm comes out of the penis and travels up to meet the egg.

If the egg is fertilized by a sperm, the woman becomes pregnant—which means she's going to have a baby!

The fertilized egg goes on down to the uterus and makes itself at home in a soft lining especially made to grow a baby in.

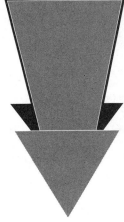

What if the egg is not fertilized?—(Which of course, it can't be if you don't have sexual intercourse.) Then, the egg and the lining shed from the uterus through the vagina. This is your period.

What is this lining in the uterus made of? Primarily blood. So, what comes out of the vagina is a small amount of bloody fluid.

Now, don't go *"Yuck!"* Blood is good stuff, not bad stuff. I mean, do you see anyone running around draining yucky, old blood out of their veins?!

"Period" blood is blood that you don't need. It's only a small amount—about half a cup. And it takes several days for it to drain out of your vagina. This is called the menstrual flow.

This flow starts very slowly, just a trickle. Then it increases for a couple of days. Next, it tapers off until it stops completely.

Now you know what all those commercials are about! Just like you use a tissue when you have a drippy nose, a woman can use several things to capture this flow of blood. Here are most of them:

• A sanitary pad or napkin. These are cotton pads that you place between your legs beneath the vagina. The pad stays there by hooking both ends to a sanitary belt, which is thin and invisible under your clothes. Sanitary pads come in many sizes and thicknesses. You can use thicker ones on days when the flow is heavier; thinner ones when that's all you need. There are pads with sticky strips on the bottom to hold them inside your panties.

• A tampon is a small roll of cotton that you put into the vagina to absorb the menstrual flow. A soft, bendable applicator lets you slip the tampon into the vagina very easily,

especially after a little practice. The tampon has strings attached to remove it with.

The nice thing about a tampon is that once it's inside the vagina, you can't feel it. Some girls use a tampon and a sanitary napkin on the days they have a heavier flow.

Girls usually keep a calendar of when they expect their next period, so they know when to tuck a few napkins or tampons in their purse, pocket or bookbag. A girlfriend, teacher, or school nurse usually has extra pads or tampons. Most rest rooms have vending machines with sanitary supplies. In a pinch, you can always use toilet tissue, kleenex, or a clean washcloth.

As a young girl, you might hear you can't use tampons. Why?

Someone might tell you it's because as long as you're a virgin (never had sexual intercourse), you have a hymen covering the opening of your vagina, so the tampon wouldn't go in. The hymen is a thin piece of skin shaped like a ring. Since the menstrual flow is coming out, it's obvious the hymen has an opening. Since a tampon is small, it can fit quite easily into your vagina.

People used to believe that the hymen was proof that a girl was a virgin. Now we know that the hymen always had an

opening, which is often stretched open even further by regular physical activity.

There have been cases of Toxic Shock Syndrome, which may be related to the use of tampons. Doctors suggest changing tampons regularly to avoid this.

These ways to absorb the menstrual flow take simple care of most of the things you might consider a "problem" about a period. After a few periods, you'll be very comfortable with using these products, knowing when and how often to change them. It's something you'll do without really thinking a lot about it.

Just like tv commercials make us look like we're all running around with body odor or bad breath, girls sometimes worry that their menstrual flow will stink. While it's true that an odor can develop if the flow is exposed to air for a long time, this really never happens as long as you change your sanitary supplies frequently.

A vaginal discharge is normal and healthy and has no bad odor. Douching (squirting water or a chemical preparation into the vagina) is really unnecessary. In fact, chemical douches and feminine hygiene sprays can irritate the vagina and vulva. The vagina cleans itself naturally. You can douche with water, but douching too often can change the normal balance of natural acids in the vagina. Wearing cotton-crotch

54

underpants and pantyhose, and not wearing your jeans so tight that the vagina can't "breathe," will help avoid any body odor from the genitals.

Remember the brain, girls. A lot of things you might spend time worrying about aren't necessary or worth it. After all, when's the last time you sat in class and thought, *"Gee, I smell so-and-so's menstrual flow"*? Or walked up to a girlfriend and said, *"Hi, I see you're having your period"*?

You might want to keep this A⁺ attitude in mind when you consider these few things that can make having a period a little bit of a pain in the neck:

• Some girls and women do have cramps, or an achy feeling low in their abdomen right before their period starts.

• Some feel sort of blah or moody or grouchy or depressed before they start their period.

• Some may feel puffy, like they've gained a couple of pounds, which is due to extra water in the body.

But don't be discouraged! Some girls have none of these pre-menstrual symptoms (PMS). Or just some of them some of the time. They might take a couple of pain relievers for cramps, cut down on salt to ease fullness from water retention, and spend one of those more miserable feeling afternoons

55

©Carole Marsh/Gallopade International/800-536-2GET/www.gallopade.com/Smart Sex Stuff for Kids 7-17

alone reading a good book instead of barking at their friends or family.

The most important thing to remember about any of these discomforts, if they occur, is that they're *temporary*. They only last a short time. And while they might be very *physical* problems—your *mental* attitude can either help you feel better about these temporary situations...or worse.

So keep your chin up! Why not? If you're going to have a period one week each month for the next 25 or 30 years, you only have two choices:

A. Make a big hassle and bothersome ordeal each month, or;

B. Experiment with sanitary products and relief for any uncomfortable problems until you discover an easy, satisfactory way to handle your period.

Once, women might have thought it was best to skip school, or work, go to bed, or otherwise give in to their period. But these days, girls and women keep right on going: to school, work, the Olympics and space!

Just like the rest of your lifetime of sexuality, this is up to *you*—so start right out with the best attitude possible and it'll become one of the best habits you ever develop.

56

Do this even if your Mom or Aunt or other female adults make a big deal over their period. They may not have heard all the things you're reading here when they were girls. It's too bad they were influenced by women who probably called a period "the curse." But there's no need for you to feel or be that way.

If you really do feel bad, don't sit around and be miserable. If you have bad cramps or other problems, your school nurse or doctor can help you.

Also, don't fall for any of those old wive's tales like "Don't take a bath during your period," and "You can't get pregnant during your period." You can do anything during your period that you can do when you are not having your period—including get pregnant if you have sexual intercourse.

When do girls start their periods? Sometimes as young as 9 or 10. Usually around 11-14. But it's quite normal for some girls not to have their first period until age 15 or 16. Girls usually have a period (as part of this complete reproductive cycle) about every 28 days. But for some women, every 20 days is normal...for others as much as every 35 days. There are new prescription medications that may even allow some women to have fewer periods each year, if they want to.

When you first begin to menstruate (have your periods), they may be irregular. One time the flow might be heavy and last for more than a week. The next time, it might be light and

57

just last for a few days. Once the hormones, which are causing the periods, get regular, your periods will settle down into a very familiar pattern, which you can pretty much count on to be "normal" for you.

Sometime in their 40s or early 50s, women stop having periods. This time, called *menopause*, also may mean irregular periods. Once the woman completes her menopause, she can no longer have children since the ovaries no longer release eggs to be fertilized. Women also do not have periods while they are pregnant.

At some point, you'll have your first physical examination by a doctor which will involve checking the reproductive organs. Either a man or woman doctor knows how to make this very comfortable.

Doctors always check a child's genitals from the time they are a baby, just like they check their eyes and ears and nose and throat. Women are very fortunate that such good exams are available to keep a check on the female reproductive organs. Regular checkups give you a chance to ask questions, double check that everything is working properly, and help establish what is normal and healthy for you, so you know when there is a change that you should ask about. That change could be bad (an infection)...or it could be good—a pregnancy that you have been waiting and hoping for.

Learn to enjoy these visits to your doctor. While it might

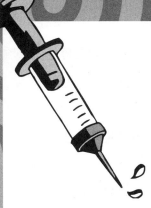

be boring to go to the doctor for a flu shot, for example, there's nothing much more exciting than going to the doctor regularly to keep an eye on a baby growing in its mother's uterus.

Then, the reasons for all this period stuff become very clear. How exciting to watch the growth of a child from something almost invisible until the time it is born. Your doctor will be as excited as you are—and just as proud.

No one understands that you have a lifetime of sex more than your doctor, and a good one will be very happy to have you as a healthy patient from a young girl right on through menopause.

A word to boys about periods: Just because you don't have them, doesn't mean you have to be silly or embarrassed or smart alecky about them. You probably don't see grown men teasing grown women about periods, do you?

No. That's a sign of maturity. Men and women talk about periods; it's no big secret. And you can go ahead and tease girls if you want to, but try to think how you'd want another boy to treat your sister or mother or daughter or you, if you were a girl.

59

No periods. One of the scariest things girls think about periods is not having one. No, I don't mean the first time. I mean after they have had them. If they miss one and have been having sexual relations with a boy, they may think they've gotten pregnant, which a missed period is often (but not always) a sign of. We'll talk more about sexual intercourse, pregnancy, contraception, etc. soon, but first we better talk about boy stuff, so we'll have both of the sexes we need before we get them together!

● ●

Indians who once lived in the coastlands of North Carolina on the eastern U.S. seaboard used a grey, stringy plant called Spanish Moss for sanitary napkins and baby diapers!

Boys, Let's Get Physical!

Whether you're a girl or boy, the time when your body is physically able to become a mother or father is called *puberty*. From the start of puberty to the time your body has reached complete physical maturity is called *adolescence*.

We've seen some of the changes this means for a girl. What about a boy?

Just like for girls, there's no automatic, set time boys begin to become men. A boy can reach puberty as young as age 10. Most boys reach puberty when they're about 13 or 14, which is about a year later than the average age of puberty for girls.

The brain is boss. The pituitary tells your body it's time for your sex glands to begin to mature. If you're impatient because your friends have a head start, or if you have left them behind—don't worry. We're all stuck with our own personal body's schedule of events. Everyone evens out sooner or later. I mean how many grown men do you see who look like little boys?

The most important thing happening to you is probably the thing you're least aware of. Your testicles are starting to produce spermatozoa, or sperm for short. The testicles also

61

produce male hormones called androgens. The androgen called testosterone causes these physical changes in your body:

1. Your testicles grow to about an inch around. The testicles are inside the scrotum, which is the sac of skin that hangs between your legs. It's normal for one sac to hang lower than the other. The testicles hang outside your body because sperm can't be produced inside—it's too **warm**.

2. Your penis grows. It's outside the body because it's designed to be put inside the female vagina to deposit the sperm that will fertilize the egg that creates a new life.

All boys are born with a foreskin or prepuce which covers the head or glans of the penis. Sometimes this skin is removed through "circumcision," which usually takes place soon after birth. This helps keep the penis clean, since smelly smegma can collect under this foreskin unless it's washed each day. In some countries, circumcision is very common; in others, it's considered unnecessary.

Just like girls worry about the size of their breasts, boys worry about the size of their penis. Just as breast size varies, penis size varies from man to man. There are a lot of myths about penis size that are not the least bit true. Here are a few of the things you should NOT believe:

62

• *The larger the penis, the more of a "man" you are.* Penis size has absolutely nothing to do with being "macho," becoming a father, or your ability to perform well sexually.

• *You can guess the size of a man's penis from the size of his hands or feet.* Not any more than I can guess the size of your ear by looking at your big toe!

• *Women prefer to have sexual intercourse with a man with a large penis rather than a small one.* Penis size is probably the last thing on any woman's list of "wants" as far as sex is concerned. The size of the penis has nothing to do with the amount of sexual pleasure you can give a woman.

You might not pay as much attention to your penis, other than to go to the bathroom, if it didn't begin to have a mind of its own!

What's it up to?

The sperm produced in the testicles moves on to a storage area called the epididymis. From there, the sperm enters the vas deferens which loops up and backward inside the body to join up with a seminal vesicle and the prostate.

In order to survive, the sperm cells mix with a milky, white fluid—semen. When the semen carrying the sperm leaves the body, it does it like this:

63

• First, the penis gets stiff and hard. This is an erection. What makes the penis get erect, or have an erection? Blood flows into the spongy tissue of the penis.

Sometimes the penis gets erect for no apparent reason. You may just be minding your own business—riding your bike or taking a shower.

Sometimes, it gets stiff because you're sexually excited— thinking about girls, or reading a magazine or watching a movie that shows love scenes or other "mushy stuff."

A man's penis also becomes erect so it can enter a woman's vagina to deposit sperm.

When an erection occurs when you don't want it to or when it may be embarrassing, then you feel pretty miserable. But erections are as common and normal as can be.

Once the penis is erect, another muscle contraction causes the semen to shoot out the end of your penis. This is an ejaculation. This is when a male has an orgasm.

Sometimes the erection goes away and the semen is not ejaculated from the body. That's okay. The semen just stays in the body until later.

You can have an erection and ejaculation at night while you are sleeping. This is very normal. It's called a seminal emission (which sounds more like something related to your car, doesn't it?)—but you've probably heard it called a *wet dream*. This is the body's way of getting rid of semen it no longer has room to store. Sometimes you may wake up in the middle of a wet dream; other times you may sleep right through it. Some boys never have wet dreams.

Even though the semen comes out the urethra, which is the same tube that urine comes out of when you go to the bathroom—urine and semen never pass through the tube at the same time.

Another time that the penis becomes erect and ejaculates semen is when you masturbate. Masturbation is rubbing your genitals until the penis is stimulated enough to become erect. (Girls rub their vulva, clitoris and vagina.) This may produce an orgasm.

What are "blue balls?" Just a colorful term to describe an ache in the groin or sex organs. This can happen when you have an erection for a long time without ejaculating. It'll go away once your sexual excitement is past. It might hurt, but it won't hurt you at all.

65

Master Bation

Why do you masturbate? It feels good. It's a natural way to learn about your body. From the time you're a baby, you're curious about how many of this you have, what this hole is for. Even though you can read books, take a biology or sex ed class, or "play doctor" with a friend—it's not the same as exploring your own body to see what's where and how it looks and feels. Don't be shy—get a mirror and look around!

Yes, people used to think (and some still do) that masturbation was bad and bad for you. But since everyone does it and it's never been known to hurt anyone, masturbation is really no big deal. It's not wrong or bad or harmful or stupid or silly or any of those things.

This personal exploration of your body and how it responds is good preparation for the time when you'll let another person touch the sexual parts of your body. It not only makes you look forward to that time, it also makes you realize what a special time that will be, and not something that you'd want to share until the right time for *you*.

Do adults masturbate? Yes.

Why? There's always more to learn about your body. Most people enjoy the sexual satisfaction masturbation can bring. While most adults probably prefer sharing their bodies with someone else, there are times in anyone's life when this is not possible or not a good idea.

66

When? Well, especially when you're too young to have sexual relations with another person. Our sex urges are very strong. Our minds know that sexual intercourse can bring pregnancy. And most kids know that a baby is something adults should have—not kids! So, masturbation is a way for us to satisfy some of our sexual needs without the risks that can accompany having sex with another person.

What kind of risks? Getting pregnant or getting a girl pregnant is the main problem. It's not a problem if you're married and settled and ready to have a family. But if you're still in school, perhaps planning on college or a job—the last thing you probably need is a baby!

Other risks include getting a disease. Just as there are colds and the flu and other contagious diseases, there are diseases that can only be caught through sexual intercourse. The disease we've been reading about the most in our world headlines these days is AIDS. But there are many other sexually-transmitted diseases.

Last, but not least, having to worry yourself sick over having sex when you feel pretty sure it's not the best thing for you to be doing at this particular time in your life.

You not only have to worry about yourself and your partner and pregnancy and disease, but also if you are going to get caught ... if you can go back to not having sex, once you start...if what you're doing is right or wrong—and an endless number of other worries that kids don't need.

As an adult you may masturbate for similar reasons. Maybe you don't want or have a steady girlfriend or boyfriend. Perhaps your husband or wife doesn't feel up to sex. You and your sex partner may be separated.

None of these things mean you lose your interest in sex. But as you can see, many times masturbation may be the most logical, easiest, safest and satisfactory outlet for your sex needs.

Well, let's leave the penis alone for now. *(Oh, you know what I mean!)* Here are some other changes that happen to you on your way to becoming a man:

3. You grow hair in the pubic area around your genitals. At first, it may be soft, straight and smooth, then, longer, darker and more curly or wiry. Hair grows under your arms, on your arms and legs, and possibly on your chest. At some point, you'll begin to grow hair on your face. The amount of hair and when a boy begins to grow it varies from boy to boy. Don't worry about it—about the time you finally get that hair on your face you may have longed for so bad, you may discover

68

that shaving everyday (if that is the custom where you live) may be more of a chore than a thrill!

4. Your voice loses its boyish sound and grows deeper. While this transition is taking place, your voice sometimes "cracks"—or starts out on a word in a deep tone, then sort of squeaks out the ending, or vice versa. This is normal and happens to everyone. Pretty soon, your vocal chords will get used to their new sound and you won't have this problem anymore.

5. Because of those active glands, you may perspire or sweat more than you used to. Normal. Normal. Normal.

6. Acne. Zits. Pimples. Blackheads. Boys and girls often have problems with acne on their face and neck. These aggravating skin problems are caused by the changes in your body, so this should be a temporary problem. Everything that helps your body—good food, keeping clean, enough sleep—helps your skin. Your doctor or pharmacist can suggest medication that might help your acne if it does not clear up.

7. Your entire body will begin to be shaped more like a man's and less like a boy's. Your shoulders grow broader. The muscles in your arms and legs develop more fully. Some soft and flabby "baby fat" you may have put on while you were growing and changing disappears.

69

You usually don't get as tall as you're going to until age 18 or 19—so give yourself time! Also, all this new growth may make you seem clumsier for a while, but pretty soon, you'll be used to (and proud of!) your handsome new body.

8. You're smart enough to know that just because your body is suddenly capable of fathering a child, and just because you discover you have a dramatic new interest in girls and sex stuff—that emotionally you may not be ready for all this!

Relax. No one expects you to be. Adults—parents and teachers and older brothers and sisters and friends—are well-aware of the emotional changes that go along with growing up. After all, they've been through all this themselves.

Some of these strong new emotions are exciting; others seem a real bother. I mean you were pretty good at thinking girls were a big pain...and now you're afraid you might actually be beginning to like them. Yikes!

Well, maybe the best way to make you feel better about all these new feelings is for us to talk a little about boys and girls together, or...

70

HOT STUFF

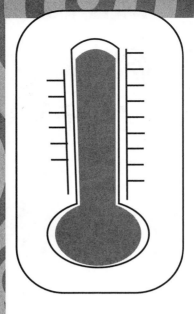

HOT STUFF!

Sooner or later, you're going to get very interested in boys or girls. It may not be sexual at first. But as your feelings change, a great interest in another person's body and wanting to have sexual relations with them is a common—and oftentimes, *very* intense feeling. Why?

Life Isn't Fair

Right! But life seems especially unfair when it comes to our sexual feelings. Most kids would agree that graduating from high school and exploring college or career should come before you settle down, get married and have children.

So, why is your body so interested in sex when you're still far too young to cope with the problems and responsibilities sex can create?

Hor(mones) Today...Gone Tomorrow

It's those "horny" hormones at work again! Peer pressure, curiosity, strong sex urges, "sexy" tv, movies, record lyrics, friends who swear they have sex, someone who says, *"If you really love me, you'd have sex with me"*, or feeling like the last virgin on Earth may *egg* you into having sex—even when you know you're too young.

If you do go ahead and have sex, who cares? Not your hormones...not the rock singers. If you get pregnant or get someone pregnant, are you going to blame the movie producers? Are your peers going to counsel you about an abortion? Will your hormones pay your hospital bill?

Sure, your parents care—but it's still *you* who has to cope with all the new considerations sex brings. Even if you don't get pregnant or get someone pregnant, you'll have plenty of other stuff to think about: contraception—your luck can't hold out forever; competition between sex and things you used to enjoy—sex takes time and birth control costs money; loss of friends—a sex partner can be very demanding; lower grades—sex and sex worries leave little time to study. *(So can a baby!)*

And your sex partner cares—at least as long as he or she enjoys the arrangement. But what if they change their mind—where does that leave you? Probably hurt. Angry. Afraid—especially if you've been having sex without any contraceptive protection. (Or, maybe even *relieved* if you've about decided you're too young for sex.)

What if you're the one who wants to break off the relationship? If your partner's angry and hurt, you may feel guilty. If your partner doesn't want to stop, you may be in for more problems than you ever imagined.

73

Even if you use contraceptives, you can still get a sexually-transmitted disease. Even the milder ones can be a real pain in the neck and other assorted places...cost money ...and require time out of school. While some can be cured, they can also leave their permanent mark in damage to your body. Some can't be cured. These can create problems you may have the rest of your life.

And, then there's AIDS—the sexually-transmitted disease that can kill you. No one really likes to talk about AIDS to kids. *Why?*

Because, believe it or not, as much as adults seem to just say *NO! NO! NO! DON'T! DON'T! DON'T!* when it comes to sex, they really do want you to think sex is a great thing—especially when it's the right time for it. Adults know sex is special—something that's fun and enjoyable. And that sex is about life—not death.

But adults have to tell you about the negative side of sex, too. And nothing in the history of sex has been as bad as AIDS. We'll talk more about AIDS in a minute. But if sex has sounded super-wonderful until now (and it is!), then it also must sound very serious. It is. *Very* serious. **Deadly** serious.

So, golly, gee whiz, phooey—how can you get interested in the opposite sex, date, cope with your horny hormones and yet still make all this work out like it's supposed to?

74

©Carole Marsh/Gallopade International/800-536-2GET/www.gallopade.com/Smart Sex Stuff for Kids 7-17

THE DATING GAME

First, dating has gotten a "bum rap." It might seem like the whole goal of dating is pairing up, going together, going most of the way, going all the way, and then going crazy if the girl ends up pregnant, or going separate ways if the boy decides that's just your tough luck...not his.

This is not really what dating is—or has to be.

Dating is this:

- *Friendship*—with the opposite sex.
- *Exploration*—of other types of people and how they act and what they think.
- *Exploration of yourself*—what you like and how you feel and what you believe.

Dating is meant to be temporary. You don't want to be friends with just one person. You don't want to learn only one person's interests, ways, or habits. You don't want to discover how you react to just one person.

Dating one person is like trying one new food. Pizza's great, but if you never tried anything else, you'd never know how super hamburgers and hot dogs and tacos and chop suey are.

75

Dating is meant to be fun—not serious. So, if dating's about meeting new friends and doing new things and having fun—what makes it seem so serious sometimes? Or rather, *who* makes it serious?

- *You, the girl:* Girls are usually ready to date before boys are, so they often "weasel" a date from a reluctant boy. Just about anything that isn't 100% agreed on by both people is usually less fun than more fun. But maybe you got what you wanted by "conniving" to get a date. Didn't you?

- *You, the boy:* Since girls are eager to date, it's pretty easy for an older boy to take advantage of the situation. You may have dated before, or even be sexually experienced, and so turn the fun date the girl expected into a wrestling match.

- *You, the boy and girl:*—who could have been perfectly happy being friends, but because your other friends are "going together"—decide to copy them. (Not much fun if you're just pretending you like each other while peeking over each other's shoulders at someone you'd really like to date!)

So, date smart. Smart dating will help you go through a more logical series of typical dating events and postpone as long

as possible that hot stuff situation of two people "going together" which means you spend an awful lot of time alone. And with your hormone friends and peer pressure to help you out, the next thing you know, you're going most of the way...all the way...going, going—gone.

Smart dating =

• *Don't be in such a hurry.* Keep a list of things you haven't even done yourself yet, much less with a date. Try to do all these yourself, or with your friends or family, before you move on to dating.

• *Don't be such a copy cat.* Just because everyone else is doing something, doesn't mean you have to. If it seems like "everyone" is going steady, and so you should too...does that also mean that when "everyone" is getting pregnant and dropping out of school that you should copy them then?

• *Go slow.* Group dating will give you some experience before you wind up in the back seat of a car with a boy or girl all alone on a dark street. There's plenty of time to move on to double dating and dating alone. Every few months you postpone something, gives you a chance to grow a little more mature.

77

• *Don't let dating be your only goal.* Sure, you want a date for the dance. But you can still go with the guys or gals to a movie. Have a hobby. A sport. Travel. A job?

• *Think about dating for the long term, not just the short.* If your whole goal is to date one person, you've sure cut yourself off from a lot of exciting options. Try to picture yourself dating during high school...when you're in college or tech school or working...and as a young adult with a career.

When you're a young dater, probably the best you can do is go to the movie or a dance or a rock concert, maybe. But the longer you date and the older you get, the more apt you are to find yourself on some pretty exciting dates: Skiing—in another country? A "barefoot" working cruise on a real sailing ship? Why not?!

Think of all the super dates you might cheat yourself out of by opting to get too serious about one boy or girl at too early an age.

If dating can be so much fun for such a long time, why do so many kids make it so miserable?

• *They get in too big a hurry.* It's easy to talk a boy or girl into going out on a date...teasing or tricking them into a situation where sex seems mighty appealing...talking them into sex. But that's not a date—that's a disaster!

78

• They worry too much about that one date.
A date can be a one time thing. If the girl or guy is
not gorgeous—so what? If you goof up and do or

say something stupid or silly—
who cares? If he or she doesn't
fall madly in love with you—will it matter
next week when you go on a date with a
great new person you just met and spend
part of the evening laughing at what a crazy
date you had the week before?

• They compete with their friends.
When you try to do everything your backseat
friends do—whether you want to or not,
all you've accomplished is to be pretty sure that whatever
problems or regrets they have, you will too.

*But what about sex and dating? Don't most kids really
end up having sex with a date sometime in high school,
almost no matter what?*

That's a very good question. In fact, it's really two
questions:

1. Don't most kids really end up having sex?

Well, here is one current statistic:

*According to the Surgeon General of the United States,
70% of U. S. teenagers are sexually active.*

79

2. Don't they end up having sex—no matter what?

No matter **what**? What is what?

- No matter if they don't want to?
- No matter if they didn't mean to?
- No matter if they knew better?

The answer is: they may end up having sex, but it will not be "no matter what." It will be because they wanted to, or thought they did, or their date wanted to and they gave in, or they "just couldn't stop themselves," or some other specific reason. They may not want to admit that at the time, or even for a long time—but some reason will be the reason—not a "no matter what."

Then why do so many kids end up having sex when it seems like it's a lot smarter and a lot more fun to wait?

Good question. There are as many answers as there are kids:

- *Immaturity:* If you put yourself in a position where sex is far more likely than less likely...if you egg or tease your partner on...if you think you can "do everything but" indefinitely—you're just kidding yourself.

- *Immaturity:* If you feel like you're the only virgin in the world...if "all your friends are doing it"...if you just can't resist and think you can later blame it on hormones or him or her—

80

you are going to get sex, but you may not get what you want.

BUT THIS IS HARD. WE'RE IN LOVE. WE WANT TO TOUCH EACH OTHER. WE WANT TO MAKE LOVE. WHY IS THAT SO BAD?

It isn't. It's unfortunate that your body tells you it wants something you really don't need for a few more years.

No, life isn't fair. But sex is a fact of life. And only **you** can be sure that it isn't a fact of your life until you want it to be. You can have all the excuses in the world after it happens, but in spite of all the obstacles to staying in control, it's still up to you.

Let's say you do reach 10th grade or 11th or 12th and have a serious relationship with a boyfriend or girlfriend. Now what?

Well, if it's really serious and you're mature enough to want to make love to one another, then you ought to be mature enough to figure out how to keep from having sex. *(If you can't, maybe you're not as mature as you think!)*

For one thing, you can sure *talk about it*. If you want to be lovers, then I sure hope you're friends. And friends help each other. Help each other avoid situations that leave you with little option but having sex.

81

Masturbate. We've already decided it isn't a bad thing at all. While you can sure overdo it if that's all you do, if it helps relieve your sexual frustration and avoid sex and all the possible complications we've talked about, then try it—and encourage your boyfriend or girlfriend to do the same.

Sex Ed: If there's not a class at your school, then try to take one together somewhere, or at least read this or another book together.

If HE knows that SHE knows that he will not die, or anything else, if he doesn't get sex—then maybe HE will lay off (instead of "on") HER.

If SHE knows that HE knows that condoms aren't really 100% percent effective as a contraceptive, then maybe HE won't want to push their luck by starting a sex relationship that means that every time they have sex, they push their luck just a little more.

ALSO: the more each of you learn about AIDS and other sexually-transmitted diseases, the more you'll both have to agree that sex is something strictly for adults—which you *almost*, but not *quite*, are.

WHEN *IS* SEX OKAY? WE KIDS AREN'T DUMB. WE KNOW THAT COLLEGE KIDS AND YOUNG ADULTS

WHO ARE WAITING UNTIL THEY ARE 25, OR 30 TO GET MARRIED ARE HAVING SEX—AREN'T THEY?

This is probably the most important question you've asked. It's only fair that if adults ask you, in fact—BEG YOU—to abstain from sex, especially while you're still in junior or high school, that they give you some clue as to when you can have sex. But, it may be your older brother and sisters, college or tech school kids, or young adults who can answer that question best.

DAVID: *"Somehow after all those wild years of hormones driving you crazy, your body gets as mature as your head. Sure, you still want sex, but you're able to relate it to other things you want too. If you're one of the lucky kids who keep their sexuality under control, you'll find it pays off later when you have a job and money and can spend it on some things you want instead of a wife or doctor bills or baby bottles. You enjoy dating even more, once sex isn't the only thing you want out of it. If you have sex, that's great, but now you're not so frantic about it. Of course, AIDS and other sexually transmitted diseases have put a real damper on casual sex. But that isn't so bad. All the reasons that casual sex wasn't a great idea in high school doesn't really change when you get older. You still don't want to accidentally get someone pregnant. You sure don't want to get a sex disease. So, you tend to have sex with someone you really care about and know. That's a lot more satisfying than a steamy, quick encounter with a girl at her house after school while you watch in a panic over your shoulder to be sure no parent is coming in the door!"*

83

SUSAN: *"If girls ever had a reason to postpone sex, they do now. Bad reasons like AIDS, and herpes, and other diseases. But so many great reasons! If you make it out of high school without being tied to some boy sexually, you can really begin to live your life. Whether you work or go to school or both—you meet people who've achieved the same things. No one's eager to mess up their opportunity to get an education, make money, travel, or start a career, by having sex with just anyone. Guys know girls really have it made these days as far as equal opportunities, so they know that getting married doesn't really influence girls like it might once have. If you thought you were saving yourself for marriage, that's great. But you also saved yourself for YOU. I'm having a great time. Sex is on my list, but I just haven't got there yet. Maybe after my next raise and trip to Australia!"*

L.J.: *"Look, things are different and adults won't do you kids any favor trying to fool you. I want to have sex. I love sex. But AIDS kills people—even young people. In fact, especially young people. No, you don't have to give up sex. But the facts of life are that we young adults don't have sex unless we know the other person really, really well. That means we know if they have had sex with a lot of other people or not. Believe me, not having been sexually active in high school is a big plus + these days! Surprise!! The person I'm dating and I have had a monogamous relationship for many years. That means we care enough about each other to be sure each other will be protected from getting a disease that can kill you. And, it means we can relax and enjoy sex. Since she's on the Pill, we don't even have to use condoms since we were both virgins before we met each other. Sex is great. But it's strictly for adults, no matter what your age."*

Well, it doesn't sound like everyone's waiting until they get married, does it? But they sure sound like they're glad they waited until after high school. And they take complete responsibility for their sex life.

84

Which leads us to one final conclusion before we find out about some serious sex stuff. And that's this:

Sex isn't "sexy."

Huh?

??? But the record album songs and covers make it sound sexy? Videos show sex is sexy? Sexy *is* sex, isn't it?

Nope.

Sexy is a guy with his shirt unbuttoned and his chest hair peeking out. Sexy is a girl in a pale yellow dress with a great tan sitting in candlelight. Sexy is wild—hot music, red plastic clothes, and jumping **up** and **down** dancing. Sexy is sweet nothings (or maybe gross words?!) whispered in your ear. Sexy is holding hands that are growing sweatier by the minute. Sexy is blue eyes beneath thick, black eye lashes.

Then, what is sex?

Sex is a physical act. It's the placing of a man's penis into a woman's vagina. It can be putting a penis into a mouth. It can be a variety of physical things, not necessarily involving anything "sexy."

85

Sweet nothings and red plastic clothes won't kill you. Sex with a person you have known for a long time and you know to be completely free from sex-diseases won't kill you.

Sex with a person you don't know, who may have had sex with others with AIDS—can kill you.

Sex can be sexy. But sexy is *not* sex. Don't confuse the two. Maybe all you want is the sexy. The excitement. The thrill of the idea of sex. Maybe you know you aren't ready for the physical act itself. Maybe it's not worth the risk. Maybe you are getting smarter by the minute, kid!

SERIOUS STUFF

SERIOUS STUFF

So far, I hope you've discovered that sex has many sides. It's physical. Mental. Exciting. Fun. Weird. Silly. Scary. Romantic. Messy. And serious.

(FIRST) AIDS

One thing about sex is *deadly* serious AIDS.

The reason AIDS gets so much attention is that it kills people. Even though there's a lot of research going on around the world, scientists do not know how long it will take to find a cure.

What is AIDS?

The letters A. I. D. S. stand for:

ACQUIRED: got
IMMUNE: as in the body's immune system which fights germs and viruses
DEFICIENCY: lack of
SYNDROME: disease or disorder

AIDS is a disease that cripples the immune system. It leaves a person susceptible (more likely to get) a variety

88

(many kinds) of infectious (very contagious) diseases.

How do you get AIDS?

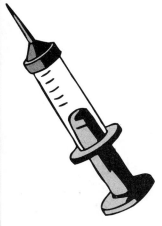

• By having sex with a person infected with AIDS.
• By using needles to inject drugs that an infected person has used.

AIDS is transmitted this way because the virus is found in: blood; semen; and vaginal secretions.

This means you can get AIDS anytime a man's semen or a female's vaginal secretions touch you and that person is infected with the virus. Since these things most commonly occur during sexual intercourse, that is the main way the disease is transmitted.

Since these things *do not* happen when you shake hands, hug, kiss on the lips, cry, cough, sneeze—you can sit by someone who has AIDS, or eat a sandwich they made, but you won't get the disease.

But if a man has sex with a woman who has AIDS, he can get it.

If a woman has sex with a man who has AIDS, she can get it.

If a man has sex with a man who has AIDS, he can get it.

If a woman has sex with a woman who has AIDS, she can get it.

And if you use a needle that someone who has AIDS has used, you can get it.

What's the difference between having the AIDS virus and the disease?

People with the virus can either have no, mild, or very severe symptoms. At least 1/4 to 1/2 of the people who get the AIDS virus will develop the disease. This happens 4-10 years after they're infected. Many scientists believe the percent of people infected who go on to have AIDS will increase as time goes by.

What are the symptoms of AIDS?

A cough that won't go away, fever and having a hard time breathing. Other symptoms can include purple blotches and bumps on the skin. The AIDS virus can also cause brain damage.

(Now, don't croak just because you have the flu or your best friend acts like a fruitcake!)

The important thing to understand is that when you have sex with another person, you're really having sex with **every** person they've ever had sex with—and one of them could have AIDS.

90

Wouldn't they know if they had a sex disease?

Not necessarily. Just as your body can carry a cold germ, then surprise you the day of the school field trip, a body can carry a sex-disease virus which may not become active until later—even though they are contagious **NOW**. And, people don't always tell the truth.

That's terrible! How can I ever trust someone enough to have sex with them? It seems too weird to have to talk about your sex life with someone you may hardly know. Plus, I'm not perfect. What if I have sex anyway? Isn't there anything I can do to be sure I don't get AIDS?

Who can you trust? Only someone who cares enough about you to wait to have sex until both of you are old enough. You can only trust someone whose sex background you know 100%. If you don't know someone well enough to talk about their sexual history —you sure don't know them well enough to have sex!

Think of your sex life as a clean slate. You want to fill that slate with good things. But AIDS is something that can't be erased from that slate.

91

Most kids, especially teenagers, begin to think about having a great sex life. That's natural. And you know that getting pregnant or getting someone pregnant can really mess up your sex life. Well, AIDS can mess up your sex life forever. **You can't have a sex life when you're dead!**

We're all human. We all make mistakes. (Of course, we make a lot fewer mistakes when we know more about something and have a chance to think *first* and act *later*—which is what sex education and this book are all about!) So, even though I say, *"If you are going to have sex with someone anyway, be sure and use a condom and spermicides"*—that doesn't sound like the kind of smart thing a person who's fixing to make a dumb mistake is going to stop and do, huh?

One thing you can think about doing is just not having sex. If you're pretty young, you will probably say, "No problem. Sounds smart. *I'm gonna wait until I get married.*"

But if you're a teenager and in love and believe all your friends are having sex, and besides, your school clinic even offers birth control if you want it—then you probably think this is the dumbest idea you ever heard. Or too hard. No fun. Maybe you could wait a month or two, or even a semester or two, but, "gosh, that's all!"

But statistics show a lot of kids have sex.

Statistics also show a lot of kids **aren't** having sex. And, this statistic is **growing!**

92

Why? Because a lot of your older brothers and sisters and young adults are deciding that NOT having sex is better. Smarter. Safer. Easier. It's not even so bad. They can still date. And hug. And kiss. And even "neck." But they're postponing the act of sexual intercourse until they are ready to have a long-term relationship with one person they know is 100% free of any sex disease. And their reward will be that they can have sex without worrying about dying.

This is a new trend. A few years ago it seems like all we read about were singles bars and sex. And NO SEX is sure not what the commercials and records and some tv shows picture. But things have changed—and pretty fast. So, where once you only had your parents to lean on you about waiting until marriage or not having sex until you were older—you might now find your older brothers and sisters and friends leaning on you even more!

Also, because you know about AIDS, and through sex education, your friends know about AIDS, you might even begin to find a little cooperation. If you had the courage or smarts to say, *"Not me—not yet"* to sex, you might even be part of helping peer pressure be **less** pressure. You may have seen this happen in relation to drugs and smoking. Why not sex?

93

No, your sex urge is not going to lessen, just because of AIDS. But, as we talked about earlier, ideas about sex change over the years. I doubt we're going to rush out and put modesty skirts on piano legs (they'd look silly in mini skirts anyway!), but I do think you can help change some attitudes now that help make sex at least a little less of a "have to", "ought to", "everybody else is" subject. Not only will you help yourself, but how would you like the general attitude to be when your younger brothers and sisters are your age? *(I'll bet you don't even want to think about them having sex!)*

What about the test for AIDS? Is it always 100% right?

Sex is like life—nothing is 100% guaranteed! If it was, people who always use contraception would never have babies—but they do!

The AIDS test is a very accurate blood test. But it's not 100% guaranteed to be correct each and every time it is given. When a person has a test that is not absolutely positive or negative, another more complicated and expensive test is given to be sure.

So, to sum up, the only sexual activity safe for a young person is:

- No sex
- Masturbation
- Dating and hugging and kissing are ok

94

• Sexual intercourse, including males and females, males and males, females and females, penis into vagina, penis into mouth, mouth on vagina, penis into anus—should be avoided to avoid any risk of getting AIDS.

Well, I think that's all the bad news about AIDS for now. I'm glad I have a lot of good things to tell you about sex and I'm sorry to have to tell you such bad and scary things. But it's very important that you know about them.

Maybe you have no intentions of having sex for a long time. That's good. It's also good that you are learning more about the facts of sex now, so you'll have this information when you need it.

You may have a girl or boy friend you're 100% certain is a virgin. And you are "probably" right. But "probably" can turn into big problems if you are wrong.

You may be older and believe you are ready for sex. You may be determined to have it no matter what a book, adult, or statistics say. But just remember, your age probably makes your situation even riskier.

If you're dating older boys, how do you know that they haven't had sex with older girls who could be infected? Or,

even if they're not homosexual, at least tried sex with another man and become infected?

If you're dating a girl and want to have sex, how can you be sure she hasn't had sex with other boys or men who are infected? Also, it's a sad fact of life that child abuse often includes an adult having sex with a child. That adult could have passed on the AIDS virus.

And even if someone tried drugs with a needle just **once**, they could have been infected.

The odds are that none of these people have any AIDS symptoms, and so may not even know they have the virus.

If you get pregnant or get a girl pregnant and you have the virus, it can be passed on to your child through the bloodstream. You would be having a child that would be infected with AIDS, who could die.

If it seems unfair or even horrible that human sex is this complicated, remember the animal and insect and bird sex lives we looked at. If those are just a few samples of how complicated sex can be for more simple life forms, it shouldn't be surprising that human sexuality offers an endless number of complications and possibilities and problems. We may not want it to be that way. But that is the way it is today.

SICK SEX STUFF

Most of the time your body works just fine—including the sex organs, inside and out. But like any other machine, your body requires maintenance. The same good nutrition, rest, exercise and hygiene that keep your hair, heart and elbow healthy, keep your sexual organs healthy.

When your body is changing rapidly, you may interpret the tiniest bump into a dreadful disease. Don't! Let your new knowledge be a source of comfort that while most of the bad things we've talked about will probably never affect you, you at least know they exist, how to avoid them, what the symptoms are, and how to check on them.

Your sex organs can have normal aches and pains. We've talked about common menstrual discomfort. A swollen testicle or itchy vagina can just as easily be the result of tight jeans as some awful disease. So don't panic—*think*.

Some things are supposed to happen! A clear, whitish discharge from the vagina is **normal**. White pimples on a penis may simply be blocked oil glands which don't mean anything. When in doubt—*ask*, don't worry.

Not all problems with your sex organs are related to sex. So don't be embarrassed to explain your symptoms and get some help—*sooner*, not later.

97

STD = SEXUALLY TRANSMITTED DISEASES

Sexually transmitted diseases means exactly that: diseases that are passed from one person to another during sexual intercourse.

A lot of kids don't think they can get any of the following diseases if they keep themselves clean, don't have sex very often, or have one, steady sex partner.

Sorry, but this is just not true. At all.

Sexually transmitted diseases can infect anyone. You can get infected the first—and only time—you have sex. You can be infected by the nicest, cleanest kid you know.

While you can help avoid getting a sexually transmitted disease by: using good hygiene, especially before and after sex—and insisting your partner does too; using condoms; examining a sex partner's genitals for symptoms; and not having sex with anyone who has symptoms—NOT having sex is the **best** safeguard.

What are these diseases?

• *herpes progenitalis*—or genital herpes. You can get this by having sex with another person, male or

female, through penis-vagina sex, or oral or anal sex. The symptoms are tiny clusters of painful, fluid-filled blisters on the labia, around or in the vagina, on the penis or around the anus. Your lymph glands may swell, muscles ache and you may have a fever.

Symptoms show up 2-20 days after you're infected and usually diminish or disappear after a few weeks. BUT, the virus is still in your body. While symptoms may never reappear, it's FAR MORE COMMON that they do.

You don't have to have sex again to trigger an attack. It can come when you are tired, sick, or under stress—such as during exams.

Before an attack and while you have sores, you can give the disease to someone else if you have sex with them.
Although some drugs help relieve the symptoms, there's no cure for herpes at this time.

• *chlamydia*- A woman may have vaginal irritation or no symptoms at all. A man will have a discharge from the penis and may have painful urination. Antibiotics are used to treat the disease.

• *gonorrhea*- Bacteria live in the warm, wet places of the penis, cervix, throat or rectum, and are transmitted through sexual contact. Males usually have symptoms 2-9 days after

they are exposed to the disease. They may have painful urination and an uncomfortable, thick, yellowish discharge from the penis. If the throat or rectum is infected, they may have a sore throat, rectal pain and itching and mucus in the bowel movements.

Women usually have NO symptoms until much later. By then, pelvic or lower abdominal pain can mean the undetected disease has developed into a more serious pelvic inflammatory disease. An untreated disease can cause sterility in women, problems with joints, and even in heart valves, in men and women. The disease is treated with antibiotic pills or penicillin shots.

Gonorrhea transmitted from the vagina to a baby's eyes during birth can make the child blind. Most hospitals put silver nitrate in newborn baby's eyes to prevent this.

• *syphilis*- is usually spread by sexual contact, but you can also get it if an infected sex organ touches an open cut anywhere on your skin. Symptoms show up in 3 stages:

First, 10-90 days after you are exposed, there might be a painless sore on the genitals, rectum, lips or mouth, that disappears in a week or two.

A few weeks or even months later, you might discover a rash all over your body. Your joints may swell, and you may feel like you have the flu. These symptoms will go away too, but you will still have the disease, so you can see why

100

it's important to have symptoms checked out immediately. If detected early, it can be cured.

It may be years before the final stage of the disease appears. You may discover you have damage to the nervous system, brain and/or circulatory systems. This damage can lead to heart problems, insanity, paralysis, and possibly, death.

A mother can give a baby syphilis. This can result in it being born dead or with deformed bones, blind, or a disfigured face.

• *condylomate acuminata*- or venereal warts, sound like something that a frog trying to make love to a rock should get, but it's not. They are caused by a virus and transmitted during sex. About a month or so, after you are exposed, you may find skin-colored, cauliflower-shaped bumps around your vagina, rectum or penis. They may itch and feel irritated.

You need to see a doctor fast. Why? Because the warts can spread fast and cover the entire genital area. A doctor will remove the warts—and you should only let a doctor do this.

There are several ways to remove them: with medication; burn off with an electric needle; or freeze off with liquid nitrogen.

• *pubic lice*- are six-legged parasites that live and lay eggs in pubic hair.

101

If you have sex with someone who has pubic lice, these "crabs" will be happy to jump right over to you! You can also get them from bedding, clothes, towels and toilet seats which have been infected.

You can tell you have crabs because you can see them and their eggs in your pubic hair. You'll also itch "where you can't scratch" something awful!

You might see tiny spots of blood on your underwear that comes from places where the lice have burrowed under the skin. If you can see this on you—you can also see it on someone else, so be sure and look before you leap into bed with someone!

Medicated shampoo and a prescription lotion are used to treat the lice, but that is only the beginning.

You must wash bedding, towels and clothes in very hot water to get rid of the lice and any eggs. Also, you can't have sex for at least a week. And, if you have sex again with the person you got them from (who maybe even got them from you?!)—you'll just get them all over again.

Is all that itching and washing and misery worth it?

• *scabies*- is caused by a mite. You can get it via sex, close skin-to-skin contact, or infected bedding, clothes and blankets. You'll know you have it from the awful itching—

102

especially at night.

Where the mite burrows under the skin, you may see red spots or raised red or gray lines. This can happen on the genitals, buttocks, breasts, hands or elbows. A prescription cream, more washing, and no sex will treat it.

• *tinea cruris*- "jock itch" or "jock rot." You can get this fungus that gives you a scaly, itchy rash in the crotch from an unwashed athletic supporter or jock strap. *Girls*, you can get it from guys during skin-to-skin sexual contact! It is treated with medication you can buy at the drug store, but if it doesn't get better, you'll need a prescription from a doctor for something stronger. You also need to dry off good after a shower or swim, wear cotton underwear and no tight jeans.

• *trichomoniasis*- is something else you can get sexually or from towels, washcloths or bathing suits.

It's an infection of the vagina or man's urethra. A woman would have a frothy, yellow-green discharge that smells bad; painful, frequent urination; itching; a red, swollen vulva; and maybe severe lower abdominal pain. Men may only have a little pain in the penis. Both partners must take pills.

It's important to remember that when you're playing with sex, you're not playing at all. It's mature, adult stuff. Most kids think of sex in relation to themselves. What will happen to me? What will I feel? What will I do if I get pregnant. What if I get herpes?

But, if you get a sexually transmitted disease, your doctor will want you to notify your sex partner or partners.

It certainly wouldn't be any fun to get a phone call from a boy or girl friend one day who says, "Hi, howareya? By the way, even if you don't have any symptoms yet, you probably have herpes, cause I just found out I do!"

It's bad enough to risk getting infected or infecting someone you care for. But for many sexually transmitted diseases, there's an even worse problem. Often the disease can be transmitted to a baby, either before or while it's being born.

The potential despair, frustration, and guilt are usually just not worth the few minutes of possible satisfaction.

WELL! None of these sound like much fun, do they? In addition to being painful, embarrassing, expensive (medicine, doctor visits, time off from work or school), they can sure mess up a prom or vacation.

Some can leave you unable to have children, are incurable, or can even kill you—which would sure mess up

104

what might have been a good sex life.

At this time, there are only 2 ways to avoid sexually transmitted diseases:

1. **Don't have sex.** If you have not had sex yet (maybe you're too young, don't want to, determined not to, or just got lucky)—then you could sure plan to avoid beginning your sex life with another person until you are definitely prepared to do "2." (See below.)

If abstaining sounds logical— great! Plan on it!!

If it sounds unlikely because you think most kids will have sex sooner or later—find a group to hang out with who really want to go on to college or work a lot more than they want to be a mother or a father or mess with sex diseases. Does it sound like they're selfish? GOOD. Selfish is a great way to be when it comes to sex!

It's your body and your life and your sex life and your decision. (If your boy or girl friend feel the opposite—that sex is ok and you are ready, then they are being selfish too; they want what they want, not what's good for you.)

The second choice may surprise you. You probably thought it would be about condoms. But it isn't.

(105)

2. **Only have sex with the same person**—over a very long time (this is usually called a "mutually monogamous relationship".)

"**Wow! My boyfriend and I love each other—we plan to stay together forever.**"
Super! How long is forever?
"**Oh, I'm sure all semester!**"

I'm sure you've figured out that the most common example of a mutually monogamous relationship is MARRIAGE. And while you might say you're ready for a long term sexual relationship with one person—you may not be ready for marriage.

Some young adult couples meet and fall in love and do have a monogamous relationship. They may live together and only have sex with each other.

So marriage and/or having sex with the same person can keep you from getting sexually transmitted diseases—AS LONG AS:
  • Your partner doesn't have any disease.
  • Your partner only has sex with you. In other words, once either of you have one sex act with another person one time, you are both open to the risks of sex diseases.

So far, 1. may sound easier than 2. and 2. may sound fine for adults. But you're a kid and don't want to get married or stick with the same boy or girlfriend for very long, and besides you're already sexually active. But, of course you want to avoid sex diseases 100%—so what can you do?

OPTION A: Each and every time you have sex, *without exception*—a condom must be used. Most couples find ways to make using one fun and part of their sex activities that in no way reduces their romance and pleasure. You can too.

You can reduce the risk even more by using a spermicide with the condom. Both of these together do **not** prevent your getting infected or infecting someone, but they **do** reduce the risk.

No way. Too messy. Too much trouble. Not romantic.

Then that leaves you with:

OPTION B: Just have sex naturally. Have sex when and where and how you want to. Don't use anything to avoid the risk of sexually transmitted diseases.

Yes, as much as no one wants to admit it or encourage it—this is certainly one of your choices and the choice many sexually active kids make.

107

BUT IF YOU WONDER WHERE THE STATISTICS ARE COMING FROM THAT SHOW MORE AND MORE YOUNG PEOPLE AT A YOUNGER AND YOUNGER AGE COMING DOWN WITH SEXUALLY TRANSMITTED DISEASES, INCLUDING THE ONES THAT HAVE NO CURE, AND THE ONES THAT KILL YOU, LIKE AIDS: THE KIDS WHO CHOSE OPTION B (SEX WITH NO PRECAUTIONS) ARE THE ONES WE READ ABOUT IN OUR NEWSPAPER HEADLINES.

Also, if you usually chose **Option A**, and do use a condom during sex, but decide not to even one time, you have just moved over and joined the "statistics" group. And, if you pick a boy friend or girl friend who have been part of the B group, you have just joined that group yourself.

"No" is not necessarily an easy choice to make and stick with. But when will you be **THRILLED** you did?

Maybe the first time you hear someone your age has AIDS that they got from having sex—especially if the kid is the one you said "No" to!

Do I sound like a party pooper? I know and I'm sure sorry. But this is indeed serious stuff. And scientists and people who don't kid around much about anything, predict it's going to get worse before it gets better.

108

If you aren't having sex, look at all the problems you can avoid by keeping that up until you are ready to marry or at least to have a very long-term relationship with one person (which would probably not be until after high school.)

The reward will be that you can have sex with the person you care for without having to worry about disease or condoms or anything else except enjoying one another. And a lot of people would say that is **definitely** worth waiting for!

PROFILE OF A STATISTIC

You may not really feel these sexually transmitted diseases refer to you. And, depending on your age and sexual status, they may not.

After all, if you're 7 or 8 or 17 or 18 and not having sex, you need to know about such matters, but you don't need to worry about them as far as your personal situation is concerned. *Who does have to worry?*

Here are a few types of people who have a greater risk of getting AIDS through sexual contact:

• *Homosexuals.* Primarily male homosexuals, since they are more apt to have different sex partners and engage in oral and anal intercourse.

• *Prostitutes*. They have a higher risk because they have a lot of different sex partners. If you have sex with someone who is or has been a prostitute (whether you know it or not), you have increased your risk of getting AIDS.

• The *promiscuous*. Even if you are not homosexual or a prostitute, if you have sex with a number of different people, you have increased your risks.

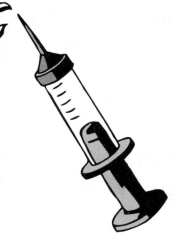

• *Drug users*. If you use a needle that someone with AIDS has used, you can become infected.

• The *younger* person having sex with older people. Your partner may have had other partners. It's just like you're having sex with them, too.

• The *ignorant*. If you don't know about sexually transmitted diseases or how to avoid or prevent them, you leave yourself open to greater risk. It's important to pay attention to new developments in this area, whether you are sexually active or not.

• The *stubborn*. The person who says, *"It won't happen to me. I'll take a chance just this once."*

(110)

SEXUAL ABUSE/RAPE

Child abuse is one of the saddest things we know about. It really seems unbelievable that anyone could hurt a child of any age. But we know that sexual abuse—even of children—is a fact of life.

Sexual abuse was one of those subjects people used to just not talk about. But now everyone knows that such problems exist.

If you are aware of or involved in a problem of sexual abuse, go to a responsible adult and tell them. The sooner you get help, the sooner the abused and the abuser can get help. Being abused is definitely something you can overcome and go on to lead a normal and happy sex life.

Who can abuse you sexually? If you are a girl, it could be a man, a boy, another girl, an adult, a child, a stranger, a parent, a date—really...anyone. If you are a boy, the same list applies. How are you sexually abused?

Rape is when someone forces you to have sex with them. It is **against the law** for anyone to do this.

We usually think of rape as being something very violent. And rape *is* an act of violence. But, that does not necessarily

111

mean that it is a dark night and someone you don't know forces you into their car and makes you have sex with them.

No matter how innocent things may start out: a date; kissing in the back seat of the car; messing around at home while your parents are at work—no one has the right to force you to have sex with them. If they do, *they* are guilty of a crime.

It's easy for us to see that when someone is forced into a car by a stranger on a dark night. But, not so easy to see when maybe you went with someone of your own free will... let them kiss and touch your body...maybe even took off part of your clothes. But, the other person still has no legal right to force themselves on you sexually or they have raped you.

They may have a hard time understanding this. *"I thought they wanted to." "They didn't say no." "You can't tease someone, then change your mind."*

But thinking someone wants to have sex is **not** the same thing as them agreeing to have sex. Not saying no is **not** the same thing as saying yes.

• You **can** change your mind. That goes for boys, as well as girls.

112

There are other kinds of sexual abuse.

• *Verbal*: such as telling jokes that put people down sexually; calling someone sexual names like "whore" or "frigid"

• *Physical*: touching someone in a sexual way without their permission (pretending it's an "accident" counts); making them touch you

• *Emotional*: threatens to say you had sex when you didn't; teases or makes fun of you for being a virgin; says they'll say you're gay, if you don't have sex with them

We usually think of sex as good, fun, clean, proper, and equal. But sex is bad when it is used to show you are stronger than another person, to make you feel good and them feel bad, to show off, to get even, to show someone who's boss, or to pay someone back, etc.

When should you think *"maybe this is sexual abuse?"*:

• When *something doesn't "feel right"*— Even a kid can tell the difference between a friendly hug and a hug that is just a sneaky way to feel your body.

• Anytime a person is older than you are, whether it's a date, parent, relative, teacher, etc.—they are sexually abusing you if:

113

• They make you do something because they know you are afraid to say no, or to leave, or to not listen

• They fool you or trick you into thinking something is okay, when it's not, that their parents are home when they're not

• When you are afraid and so give in or say yes out of fear

• When anyone threatens you, or says something is a "secret" and not to tell your parents

What can you do about sexual abuse?

You can find out more about it. You can think ahead what you'd do in different situations. Maybe you can practice "speaking up" in the mirror or with a friend or with your family. Even the shyest person can learn to say, **"No!"**—and *GO!*

Avoid putting yourself in an abusable situation. If you date a boy who is known to try to "score" on every date...if you don't stop your cousin the first time he squeezes your breast... if you go to a party where the parents aren't home...if you go "almost all the way" to tease—you have left yourself open to possible sexual abuse.

Talk with your parents about what you should do in various "tough" sexual situations. If it is a rape, you may feel

114

you have to give in just not to be hurt in any other way. This may be the smartest thing you can do.

If you are with a guy your age who seems intent on doing more than kissing when that's all you want to do—maybe you should develop a fast case of "pretend" diarrhea...or swear you are sick and are going to throw up—and say this convincingly while you are jumping up and going out the door!

Sexual abuse or rape is not something that is your fault or that you made happen. The way to avoid either is to understand how easy and fast it can happen in your own home or on a date. Imagine yourself in such situations and plan ahead how you would respond. Then try to avoid any situation that could make you a target for such abuse.

Date rape drug: Note that one way girls get into trouble is drinking something a boy has "doctored" with some kind of drug that makes you lose you inhibitions and do something you would not normally do—such as have sex. The boy may think this is a joke, or may do this just to get you to have sex. No, you will not know the drug has been added to your drink, or taste it. So, later, when you found out you had sex with someone you hardly knew or don't even like, that will be bad; it will be too late. So always look out for yourself and be

115

cautious. If something or someone or a situation just doesn't feel right, it probably isn't—get away, go home, ask for help.

Internet Predators: Another new wrinkle under the sexual sun are people who hide behind the anonymity of computers to trick girls or boys into thinking that they are  kids of the same age. Such a computer relationship may start out innocently (at least on your part), but such predators are experts at winning your trust and via the Internet "wining and dining" you until they convince you to meet them. At that time, you may discover that they aren't "a nice guy" at all, but, indeed, a grown man up to no good. Such activities have been widely reported on the news. If your parents set limits on your Internet use, that's a good thing. Even smart kids have easily been tricked and find themselves in a very bad situation. **NEVER** go and meet someone you have only "met" on the Internet.

Teachers and other adults: While it is rare that a teacher molests or rapes a student, it does happen. Again, you know when you feel something is not right and it is **NEVER** right for any adult (but especially a teacher or anyone who is supposed to be looking out for your welfare) to trick, tempt, tease, or otherwise get you to have sex with them. This is

116

AGAINST THE LAW. Sure, you can have a crush on your cute teacher; that's ok. But it's not ok for a teacher to "come on" to you. If this happens, tell a parent or other responsible adult. On the other hand, **NEVER** blame an adult for something they did not do just because you are angry or upset or got a bad grade or want to get back or get even. Then you will be the one in trouble.

"Child" molestation: You might need to know that rarely, but sometimes, a boy as young as age 10 might actually molest a younger child. This, of course, is not a good thing. If you ever witness or suspect something like this you should speak up. It has been known for children as young as 1 or 2 or even babies to be molested. Please be part of the solution to such sad and awful problems. In these instances, the molested need protection and help, and the child who is the molester certainly needs help as well.

"Hooking up": this is a new expression where friends have sex with friends, no strings attached, meaning just to have sex, not because "they're in love," etc. Yes, you might know this friend, but you do not know all about them. How do you know who else they have "hooked up" with? This is not really a very good idea.

117

Oral sex: A lot of kids think that having oral sex (usually girls sucking on a boy's penis) is not "real sex." Well, no, it's not "sexual intercourse," but it is "sex." You can't get pregnant, but as my mother would have said, "How do you know where that thing's been?!" You don't, not really, and sexually-transmitted diseases can be gotten through oral sex. *(Also, while oral sex might make the boy feel good, uh, girls, what's in it for you? Sounds like selfish sex to me.)*

The point is that most people are good. But when someone is up to no good, they are always finding new ways to trick the innocent into a situation where they may find themselves at risk of being molested or raped. This is just one reason parents like to keep an eye on their kids, adults should be present at parties, and other such things. You know it doesn't really matter that you don't like that or that you feel adults are "in your face" or "in your space"—it's their job to look out for you. So complain if you want to (that's natural), but be glad someone cares. As you get older, you will take on more of this responsibility for yourself. But in the meantime, let good folks help look out for you, and be a friend: friends try not to let friends do stupid things, especially not things that can lead to some of the bad situations we've just discussed here. I'm counting on you to be safe, smart, and wise. That's what "maturity" is and being grown up, so don't just say you are—show it.

118

PREGNANCY

One of the most serious things about sexual intercourse is that it can result in a new life. No matter how you feel about pre-marital sex, or contraception or anything else—you would probably agree that being part of the creation of a new human is a serious event. Even married couples who decide they are ready to have a baby undertake this responsibility with grave seriousness.

Maybe it seems strange that something as important as getting pregnant is so easy. You don't need lessons or a license. While it may take most of your teenage years to get your full heighth, grow a beard or breasts—one of the earliest things that happens to you during puberty is that you are able to get, or get someone, pregnant.

Can I get pregnant the first time I have sex? With clothes on? If I'm not married? Can I get pregnant standing up? Or wearing heels? Or during my period?

YES! You can even get pregnant using condoms or taking the Pill.

The most important thing to know about getting pregnant is that it will change your life—forever. Whether you have a miscarriage, abortion, keep the baby, put it up for adoption—it doesn't matter; you'll have to live with your decision.

If you're a boy, the same thing applies. Even if you don't marry the girl...or if you do...or if the mother has a miscarriage or abortion, it's still your child and you will have to live with the consequences. You have not just changed two lives—you have changed three. For the baby also has to accept consequences of your decisions. And, if *you* were the baby, you'd say, *"That's serious!"*

EXACTLY how does a girl get pregnant? Let's be very specific. As you've learned, when the boy's penis ejects semen into the girl's vagina, sperm travel up to meet an egg, and when they do, she is pregnant.

Don't kid yourself - sperm are pretty squiggly stuff! If some semen leaks out of the penis near the vaginal opening, those squirmy sperm can still sometimes find their way into the vagina. How many sperm are in a drop of semen? *Millions!* How many sperm does it take to fertilize an egg? **One.**

Also, when a boy learns his girlfriend is pregnant, he might say, *"But I used a condom—every time!"*

Condoms (or any other kinds of contraceptives) are not 100% effective 100% of the time. There can be a tiny hole in the condom that you can't see. You might put it on, but after

120

some semen has already leaked out. Or semen can escape if it accidentally comes off.

In other words, **any** time you have sexual intercourse, you are risking pregnancy.

Sometimes the only difference between a girl who is in school, maybe working part-time so she has money to travel and have fun ...and the girl who is having to work at any job to support a baby—is not money, or background, or luck, but just that one didn't get pregnant and one did.

Sometimes the only difference between the girl who got pregnant and the girl who didn't is that one had sex and one did not; or, if both had sex—one used contraception and one did not.

Boys are discovering that they can't always just walk away. Once upon a time, a boy was forced to marry the girl. In America, we call it a "shotgun wedding." In more recent times, boys could tell a girl it was too bad she was pregnant, and he was sorry, but he couldn't do anything about it, *"Because I just gotta go to college."*

Now, boys are being legally forced to accept their responsibility. Even if you don't marry the girl, you may have to support the baby until it's 18 years old—or, in other words,

121

give part of every paycheck you ever get **until you are in your 30s** to help support your child.

What if I do get pregnant?

You can have the child and keep it and raise it yourself, with its father, or with the help of your family.

At first glance, this might sound like a simple solution—so why worry? But the financial (babies are expensive!)...physical (it's exhausting to raise a young child, especially if you have to work too)...and emotional (arguments, conflicts, lack of freedom and much, much more) considerations make even the "best" of the choices full of problems.

You can give the child up for adoption or have another family member raise the child. Even though these solutions might help you stay in school and live your life a little more like you would have if you hadn't had a child—it's still your baby that will live in your heart and mind, even if you never see it again.

One of the most controversial things related to sex you will ever hear discussed is *abortion*. Abortion is when a pregnancy is stopped on purpose. This can only be safely done for the mother during the first 3 months of the pregnancy.

An abortion involves destroying the fetus that is living

122

and growing in the girl's uterus. While most people agree this can be the best thing to do under certain circumstances (the girl was raped, or her life is in danger from the pregnancy)—most people also agree this is not a good option otherwise.

Many people believe that this is killing a baby. You will need to learn more about abortion and make your own decision regarding this issue. But the one thing everyone agrees on is that abortion is **NOT** a substitute for birth control.

Like everything else, when you're trying to truly decide how you feel about a particular subject— put yourself in the other person's shoes. If you were the fetus, how would you feel? The doctor? The father? The mother?

Gee, maybe it's time to at least consider not having sex, or if you are already sexually active, getting serious about contraception. You're getting smarter every minute!—So, let's go to . . .

123

Abstinence-Only Funding

The U.S. government is currently funding an abstinence-only program that is failing American teens. Even as state after state refuses funding for abstinence-only education, Congress continues to increase the budget.

SMART STUFF

SMART STUFF
"Abstinence Makes the Heart Grow Fonder"

Well, you knew it was coming, didn't you? That somewhere in this book I'd give a big pitch for you just plain not to have sex until...until when?

Well, I could say not until you're married or 21 or mature or all sorts of deadlines. But since this book is for ages 7-17, how about not until you get out of high school? After that, you'll be 18, or close to it, and far more able to make mature decisions and accept the consequences.

Sex is a wonderful and beautiful thing with the right person at the right time. Corny—but true. Just ask the person who has tried it both ways, and they'll tell you there's a BIG difference between sex when you know it's not right for you or the other person (no matter what your body tells you!) and sex when it's intertwined with love and commitment, backed up by age and maturity. Now, that's when sex is fun and special and great!

When is the time to make a decision about not having sex until you get out of high school? Well, it sure isn't once you're in the back seat of a car with someone you think you're madly in love with!

126

The time to decide is long before then. Even if you aren't 100% sure you won't give in and have sex sometime before you finish school, hopefully there are a couple of reasons why you'll at least postpone sex as long as possible.

Make two lists.

1.
The good things that can happen if you wait on sex.

2.
The bad things that can happen if you have sex.

Sticking to your decision won't always be easy. Your body won't help you; your friends may not. That older boy who really thinks he can give you one more beer and talk you into anything couldn't care less about your list, decision or virginity! That girl who thinks she's hot stuff and can go all the way, but stop short of intercourse, is just kidding herself.

TV and movies won't help—they just make it look like sex is everything, no matter what your age. Parents may not even help if they are so suspicious that you feel like you might as well be doing what they *think* you're doing.

127

There's no one to help you except you and your main sex organ—your brain! If you refer to your lists regularly, you'll find they get ingrained in your mind.

Talk about love affairs! Your brain loves your cute little body and your body adores your beautiful brain. They will help each other all they can, especially if you help them.

The one thing you can be pretty sure about the lucky guy or gal who has a high school diploma and has just started college or tech school and has a part-time job and big plans for the future and a fun trip planned for the weekend is this:

1. They didn't have sex in high school.
2. If they did, they must have used contraceptives each and every time.

If you think I should add:
3. They got lucky! *Sorry—but statistics show that most kids just don't get THAT lucky!!*

What if you're afraid you're going to change your mind? Easy! Just take your list of reasons not to have sex and put a check (meaning *"happens"*) beside each one. Now, take your list of plans and dreams and scratch through each one!

I'm not dumb. I know that no list is going to keep a kid from having sex.

128

But not thinking ahead about it...assuming that you will have sex...not making even a tentative decision not to have sex—leaves you too wide open to circumstance and peer pressure. Not deciding **NO** is not really the same as deciding *YES*, but it sure leaves you without much will power to avoid those situations that can make not having sex just that much harder.

If you decide not to have sex and you don't, you can still date and kiss and fall in and out of love with a million boys or girls. You don't have to tell anyone your decision. You've probably already figured out that kids are going to give other kids a hard time whether they do or don't do sex, drugs, or anything else. That's what kids do.

What about *"abstinence makes the heart grow fonder?"* I believe it does.

It can sure make you grow fonder of yourself. At some point you'll decide you're pretty proud of your decision and your will power. If you avoid having sex until you get out of high school, you know you can accomplish just about anything!

And if you love someone for real— waiting can make your love grow. You can be 100% sure that the person who says, *"If you really love me—you'll make love to me"* **does NOT love you.**

129

If they did, why would he or she be willing to check off all those bad things on *your* list and scratch through all the good things on *your* list?!

If you date a lot and avoid those tough situations that make sex too easy or unavoidable—and have some "escape" ideas in case you get caught in a bad situation—any real threat to your decision may never even come up.

If you do find someone you think you really care for and feel you might end up going together awhile and even falling in love—try to find out as early as possible how they feel about sex. If they think it's ok, you might want to look around some more. Why fight that temptation if you don't have to?

If you find a boy or girl who thinks like you do, it still might not be easy—especially if you're in love. But, then maybe you can stop in the middle of some heavy necking and read each other your lists!

Even if you don't want to stop, maybe they'll feel a little bit bad about ([INSERT CHECKMARK HERE] - getting you pregnant) and (X - scratch-college) and slow things back down to a controllable level.

It's silly to even picture two half-naked kids doing this! You'd both probably laugh so hard you couldn't do much else?

130

If the going gets rough, the longer you can stick to your NO decision, the better.

At least for *this* time . .

This semester . . .

This year . . .

The Ins & Outs Of Contraception

Contraception is really the attempt to prevent 2 things:

1. Pregnancy

2. Disease

If you're a kid who has sex you MUST be concerned about both pregnancy and disease. You MUST be concerned about AIDS. And you must be concerned ENOUGH to use a condom and spermicidal foam each and every time you have sex—no exceptions, and use them in the proper way at the proper time.

(131)

Here are the various types of contraceptives available today:

1. *Condom or "rubber"*—a thin balloon-like sheath the boy puts on his erect penis. Unless the condom has a tip, leave a little space at the end. When you ejaculate, the semen goes into the end of the condom instead of the girl's vagina.

It is even more effective as a contraceptive when used with foams or spermicides (see below).

You can get condoms at the drug store or pharmacy, from vending machines in rest rooms, and from clinics that dispense contraceptives. Some schools even give out condoms.

But condoms are not 100% safe. They can be defective, with a small hole or slit in it you can't see. They can break.

Unless you hold onto the condom and pull your penis out of the vagina before you lose your erection, the condom can slip off and spill semen in the vagina.

The most common reason that couples who rely on condoms still end up having a baby or a disease is this: they decide not to use it *"just this one time."*

2. *Spermicidal foam, cream or jelly* are chemical contraceptives you put into the vagina right before intercourse.

The boy using a condom and the girl using a spermicide in the proper way is the most effective use of these contraceptives.

132

That way you are both taking responsibility; both protecting yourself and the other person; and both a little safer in case the other person forgets, or uses their contraceptive improperly, or their contraceptive does not work "that one time."

3. The *"pill"*- is really *"pills."* A girl takes a pill (usually each day) according to the directions on the package.

These are called "birth control pills" because they help prevent pregnancy. But, they do not protect you from possible disease.

How do they work? The chemicals in the pills keep your ovaries from releasing an egg each month. No egg = nothing for the sperm to fertilize.

The pills do not keep you from having your period. And, they only work if you take them. If you do not *always* remember to take them—you will not *always* be protected.

While there may be some aggravating side effects to taking the pill such as weight gain, spotting between periods, nausea—there's also the possibility of high blood pressure and other problems.

A girl who's healthy and doesn't smoke has less risks from taking the pill than from pregnancy and childbirth.

Pills are available by prescription from a doctor, family planning or school clinic.

4. *IUD (Intrauterine Device)*—a small, flexible piece of plastic that comes in different sizes and shapes. It may be coated

133

with copper or hormones and must be put into the girl's uterus by a doctor. While they're sometimes used by people who are very sexually active, they can have a lot of problems. These include not being put in correctly, falling out, heavy periods, cramps and infections. Since some problems with IUD's can leave you unable to have a baby, the IUD is not usually recommended for girls.

5. *Diaphragm*—a soft, bowl-shaped rubber cup which must be fitted by a doctor. You put spermicidal jelly on it and slip it into the vagina until it covers the cervix to keep sperm out. It has a little rim or edge around it that you tug to pull it out. The diaphragm has to stay inside you for at least 8 hours after intercourse. It's safe. It can be messy. You have to use it every time. It can get a hole or tear, so you have to check it. It can slip off the cervix during sex. If you don't have sex very often, a diaphragm can be a good contraceptive choice.

6. *Contraceptive sponge*—a small sponge filled with spermicide you put into the vagina until it fits against the cervix. It comes in one size, can be bought without a prescription, and is easy to use.

You can put it in up to 24 hours before you have sex, but it must be left in at least 6 hours afterwards.

The spermicide stops the sperm; the sponge blocks the sperm and soaks up semen. It has a small loop you pull to remove it. Some people can be allergic to the strong spermicide in the sponge.

7. *"Rhythm"*—Maybe you've heard the song, "I've got rhythm...you've got rhythm"? Well, some people who use rhythm as a birth control...also got a baby!

Rhythm is using a calendar to try to determine when you ovulate, or release an egg. If this sounds like a lot of "guesswork," it is. Even when you keep up with the exact dates of your period for many months, you still can't be sure exactly when ovulation will occur.

Rhythm is safe and has no side effects. But, it's not something you can count on to be sure you don't get pregnant.

8. *Sterilization*—could be called a "permanent" form of birth control. In other words, if you are "sterilized," you will never be able to have children.

Obviously, this form of contraception is for people who have all the children they want.

When a man is sterilized, it's called a *vasectomy*.
This is a simple operation done in the doctor's office. A small section of the vas deferens tubes are cut and tied so that no sperm can get through.

This does not affect a man's sex drive or ability. The semen he ejaculates will just not have any sperm in it. It takes about 10-15 ejaculations after the operation before all the sperm built up is released, so he is not "instantly" sterile.

135

When a woman is sterilized, it's called a tubal ligation or *"having her tubes tied."* The Fallopian tubes are cut to keep the egg from making its way from the ovary to the uterus. This is done by the doctor in the hospital or clinic. The operation can be done through the vagina or through the wall of the abdomen.

I CON...IF YOU (CON)DOM

*What's the big deal about condoms, anyway? Why, if there are so many kinds of birth control, do we hear so much about condoms, condoms, condoms? Even for **girls** to buy!*

Because only the condom can reduce the chance of pregnancy and the risk of getting or giving a sexually transmitted disease.

Sure, there will probably be a cure for AIDS one day. But there isn't now. And although there are lots of plans for future birth control, including a Pill for guys, ultrasound waves, and even contraceptive nose sprays!—you have to deal with the limits and realities of today.

Peer Pressure Pros & Cons

Peer pressure is a real hassle, isn't it? If your peers are your friends, how come they try to get you in so much trouble?

What *are* the pros and cons of peer pressure?

The *"pros"* are that if you go along, you won't be different. Nope. When your friends lie dead on the highway after driving and drinking, you'll be right there with them. When your best friend gets pregnant, why you can both drop out of school together! You won't be left out.

And if your girl or boy friend finds out they have herpes, you have one more thing in common! You'll still be part of the crowd!

Huh?

Right! There are no *"pros"* when it comes to peer pressure—there are only **"cons."**

Would you rather die of embarrassment—or AIDS? Be "different"—or "pregnant"? Be called "gay"—or be "poor" from paying child support?

Where will your best friend be (who teased you for being a virgin) when you're in the doctor's office or delivery room? Probably off on a fun weekend to check on a college near the beach!

137

SIX SMART SEX STEPS: For Virgins

If I find myself being tempted, teased, or threatened into sex, **I WILL:**

1. Do what I would I want my younger brother or sister to do!

2. Do what would I **honestly** want my own kid to do!

3. Do what will make tomorrow **better**—not worse!

4. Do what I will be **very** happy/relieved/proud I did, in the morning, in a week, next month, *in nine months!*

5. Do what I/Me/My own **real** self really and truly wants to do and knows is *best* for me!

6. Just say No, not do it, chicken out— **JUST FOR THIS TIME!**

SIX SMART SEX STEPS:
For the Sexually Active

If I think I might have sex, have sex one time, or have sex regularly: **I WILL:**

1. Prepare **AHEAD OF TIME** to protect myself against pregnancy and disease.

2. Ask my partner about their sexual history and decide if I'm hearing the **truth** or *not.*

3. *INSIST* a condom and spermicide are used, and be ready to provide both, or **STOP.**

4. Be **sure** my partner and I know how to contact one another in case either develops symptoms or tests positive for a sexually transmitted disease in the future.

5. Watch myself for *any* symptoms of disease since I'm aware this **is** a possibility as long as I am sexually active.

6. Have any symptom checked **immediately** since I know even if it "goes away," that *doesn't* mean the disease is gone.

139

LOVE

Gee, let's talk about something good for a change! Love is good. People love you (even people who don't know you)—and that's why they're concerned about your sex education, health, outlook, ideas, organs, and life.

Sex between two people who are in love is good. But love is not enough.

Even kids in love can get pregnant. Even kids who love each other a whole lot can pass on a sexually transmitted disease. Even someone who loves you can go off to college and leave you alone to have a baby and raise it as best you can.

Sometimes controlling your sexual urges is easy, until love enters the picture. You think you are in love. You believe someone loves you. You love the idea of being sexy. You love the idea of romance. You love the thought of making love to the one you love. You may even love the idea of having a baby.

Love is good, but it does not prevent pregnancy or disease or your having to suffer the consequences of either.

Love *yourself* first.

140

TRUST

Who can you trust? That's a hard question. While it might seem like you can always trust an adult—that's not true if that adult is trying to put a hand down your pants! But you can trust adults who care about kids... who care about you. You probably know exactly which adults you can trust. And, sooner or later, you learn the ones you can't trust.

How about kids? You can trust some kids; not others. You can trust some kids some of the time. You can trust your best friend most of the time, unless he or she wants you to do something they know isn't right, but they want you to do it anyway.

Frankly, it's really hard to trust a guy who says he's in love with you and would never do anything to hurt you. I mean, which is stronger—his love...or his hormone-gone-haywire sex urge?

The same for a girl who says she's "on the Pill and of course you are both ready for sex, I mean don't you love her?" Maybe. But do you **trust** her? Is she really on the Pill? Did she take them? Is she trying to trick you into having a baby and marrying her?

141

Can you trust yourself? Most of the time. You can sure trust those feelings inside you that you know are telling you the truth—even if you don't like what you hear. And with a little practice, you'll learn to trust your own judgment...your own will power...your own ability to say NO.

What about those times you can't trust yourself? We all have those times when we know we are confused. Our judgment is jumbled. Our will power is weak. No matter how much our sex organ brain says NO...our sex urges say YES!

For those times, you need a friend, adult or kid, you can trust to turn to. Maybe you can turn that face in the mirror into a trusted friend long enough to talk yourself out of something that even in your confusion, you know isn't right for you.

And you can always trust your own self when you are honest with you. If you've always done one way and now you are doing the opposite—you can kid others, but you can't kid yourself!

MORALS & ETHICS

Right and wrong. We may not always be able to define it, but we sure know it when we see it!

It's a good thing the world is so conscious these days about human rights and openness.

No matter how much immorality or unethical conduct you may see, hear, or read about, what good would it do to say, *"See! I told you. How do you expect me to do right when others don't?"*

But the headlines don't show the faithful husband, the honest businesswoman, the dedicated teacher—and they're all around you setting examples everyday.

You know what's right and wrong—especially for you. And you want others to treat you the same way they want you to treat them—no matter what the rest of the world is doing.

FULL CIRCLE

Have you ever been to a cafeteria where food revolves on a big server— when something comes within your reach you want, you put it on your tray?

If your eyes are bigger than your stomach, your tray may overflow. You may be afraid someone else will grab that great-looking piece of chocolate pie before you do.

You may be so undecided about what you want that you let the wheel of food go around several times before you make up your mind.

Your lifetime of sex is a lot like that. It's not really a straight line, but a circle. You start out rocking in a cradle, not a bit concerned about sex. And 99 years later, you will rock on the porch with the same lack of concern.

But in between, there are lots of sexual milestones to rock you. Some you have no control over. Like that wheel of food, your body is going to keep right on moving—and growing and changing from a child, to a teen, to an adult.

Everyone is faced with the same sex choices. To skip it on the first few go-arounds...to take on more physical and emotional sex than you can handle...to select what's good for you...or to choose the same thing your friends do or what someone else tells you to.

When you're presented with so many choices at once, it can be hard to make up your mind. And we never outgrow that temptation to have dessert first!

But if you can think of your lifetime of sex as a circle, you'll know that if you're patient, you can choose what you really want for you...when you want it.

I wish for you a lifetime of sex that is a circle full of wonderful things.

I know you can make it so. And so do you!

144

NEED MORE INFORMATION, HELP?

Try the following:
- Your mother or father: They may surprise you!
- Your older brother or sister: They've been there!
- Your school counselor, sex ed, or health teacher: It's their job to help you.

- Your school nurse or school clinic: They can be your special friends!
- Toll Free HOT LINE Numbers: You'll see some on tv, check your phone book, call your local information operator or the toll free operator at 1-800-555-1212, or call your local public librarian—she has a directory of numbers.

- Check your phone book for your town or state Planned Parenthood Association.
- Check your phone book for your city, area or state Teen or Adolescent Clinic.
- Check your library, bookstore or clinic for other Carole Marsh **Smart Sex Stuff For Kids**™ **Series** books. There's a listing at the end of this book. (Teachers, you have permission to copy this list.)

145

SMART SEX STUFF FOR KIDS™

GLOSSARY/INDEX

Abortion, 25, Stopping a pregnancy before a baby is born

Abstinence, 126, Choosing not to do something

Adolescence, 61, Pre-teen thru teen years

Adultery, 38, When you are married, having sex with someone else that you're not married to

Age (for sex), 26, After high school

AIDS, 26, A disease you can get from having sex; it can kill you

Anorexia, 47, Dieting to the extent it makes you very sick

Anus, anal, 36, Opening your bowels move from

Baby, 35, What kids who have sex often end up with

Birth control, 26, Ways to try to prevent pregnancy

Bisexual, 36, Person who has sex with the same and the opposite sex

Brain, 128, Your main sex organ

Breasts, 44, Glands on a girl's chest; used to feed milk to a baby

146

Bulimia, 47, Overeating and then vomiting to try to stay thin

Celibacy, 38, Deciding not to have sex

Cervix, 134, Opening to the uterus

Chlamydia, 99, A sexually transmitted disease

Circumcision, 62, The removal of the foreskin of the penis

Clitoris, 47, Small bump of flesh in the female genitals

"Come", 28, Slang word for semen or an orgasm

Condom, 82, A thin piece of rubber over the penis to contain sperm

Contraception, 73, Ways to try to prevent pregnancy

"Crabs", 102, Tiny bugs in pubic hair; lice

Cramps, 57, Aches in the abdomen before a girl's period

Dating, 75, Going out with someone of the opposite sex for fun and friendship

Diaphragm, 134, A rubber cup that fits over the cervix to keep sperm out

Douching, 54, Squirting water into the vagina to clean it

Drugs, 37, Chemicals that can kill you

"Ear" sex, 37, Paying to have someone talk sexy to you on the phone

Egg, 35, In the female that combines with a sperm to make a baby

147

Ejaculation, 65, When semen squirts from the penis during a male orgasm

Erection, 39, When the penis gets stiff and hard

Ethics, 142, Generally agreed-upon rules people follow to have a better society in which to live and work

Father, 63, What you become if you get a girl pregnant

Foam, 132, A contraceptive you squirt in the vagina before sex

Friends, 15, People who don't try to pressure you into having sex

Fun, 22, What you can have a lot more of a lot longer if you don't have sex!

Gay, 25, A homosexual

Genitals, 36, The sex organs on the outside of your body

Gonorrhea, 99, A contagious sex disease

Herpes, 99, A contagious sex disease

Heterosexual, 35, A person who prefers sex with someone of the opposite sex

Homosexual, 36, A person who prefers sex with someone of the same sex

Hormones, 43, Chemicals that cause your body to change and grow

Horny, 72, Feeling like you want to have sex

Hymen, 53, Thin piece of skin that partly covers the opening to the vagina

Immaturity, 80, Acting childish—no matter what your age

Intercourse, 26, The putting of the penis into the vagina

IUD, 133, IntraUterine Device; used for contraception

Jock itch, 103, Rash in the pubic area

Kinky sex, 37, Unusual sex acts between adults

Labia, 99, Lips of flesh in the female pubic area

Lesbian, 36, Female homosexual

Love, 15, Intense affection and sexual attraction to another person

Marriage, 84, Commitment to be sexually faithful to one another

Masochist, 37, Person who gets sexual pleasure from pain

Masturbation, 30, Rubbing your sex organs for sexual pleasure

Maturity, 126, Acting grown up—no matter what your age

Monogamy, 13, Only having sex with the same person all the time

Mother, 54, What you will be if you get pregnant and have a baby

Menopause, 58, When a woman quits having her periods

Morals, 142, Beliefs about right and wrong

Nipples, 44, Tip ends of the male or female breast

"No!", 25, A very important word in your sexual vocabulary

Normal, 111, What you are!

"Old Wive's Tales", 57, Things people say about sex that aren't true

Oral sex, 118, Sex using the mouth and the genitals

Orgasm, 64, A good feeling that can happen during intercourse or masturbation

Orgy, 37, A group of people having sex

"Outercourse", 31, Necking and petting, but not ending with sexual intercourse

Ovaries, 58, Where the eggs to make a baby come from

Ovulation, 51, The release of one of these eggs

Parent, 28, What you will automatically have in common with your Mom or Dad if you have a baby

Peer pressure, 26, People your own age who try to get you to do things you both know you shouldn't so you can all get in trouble together

Penis, 35, The male sex organ outside the body

Period, 49, The female menstrual cycle

Pill, The, 133, Taken to try to prevent pregnancy

PMS, 55, Pre (before) Menstrual (period) Syndrome (symptoms)

Pregnancy, 15, The fertilization of the female's egg by a male's sperm and the 9 months it takes for this to grow into a baby

Promiscuous, 110, Having sex with different people

Prostitute, 110, Person who gets paid to have sex

Puberty, 61, The time of your sexual development

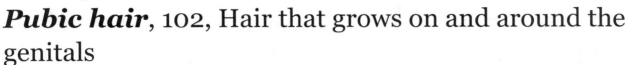

Pubic hair, 102, Hair that grows on and around the genitals

Rape, 111, The forcing of someone to have sex when they do not agree to it

Reproduction, 31, The creating of new life through sex and pregnancy

Responsibility, 21, What you must take for your sex life

Rhythm, 135, Trying to not get pregnant by not having sex on the days you think you might be most likely to get pregnant

Romance, 107, What many young people really want instead of sex

"Rubber", 132, A slang name for a condom

Safe Sex, 13, For ages 7-17, no sex

Sanitary napkins, 53, Throw-away pads a girl wears during her period

Scabies, 102, a disease that can be transmitted sexually

"Score", 114, Slang term for getting someone to have sex with you

Scrotum, 62, The sac of skin the male testicles are in

Selfish, 118, Something good to be when it comes to sex

151

Toxic shock syndrome, 54, Rare but serious medical problem that can come from using very absorbent tampons

Transsexual, 36, Person who has the physical sex organs of one sex, but emotionally is the opposite sex

Transvestite, 14, Person of one sex who likes to dress up like the opposite sex; usually men who like to wear women's clothes

Trust, 41, 65, Something or someone you can count on

Unfair, 96, What it seems like life is sometimes

Urethra, 65, Opening you urinate from

Uterus, 59, Place in female where baby grows until it is born

Vagina, 51, Opening between girl's legs that goes to the uterus

Vasectomy, 135, Sterilization of the male by cutting the tiny tubes that sperm goes thru

Venereal warts, 101, Contagious bumps on the genitals

Virgin, 53, A boy or girl who has never had sex

Vulva, 54, The outside parts of the female genitals

Wet Dream, 65, Ejaculation during sleep

Withdrawal, 154,Trying to take the penis out of the vagina before any sperm gets into the vagina

You, 66, The most important person in the world

Youth Clinics, 25, Places you can call or visit and get good information and advice about sex from nurses and doctors who won't fuss at you

Zits, 69, Slang word for acne, pimples, exzema, or other bumps you get on your face, usually before a date!

smart sex stuff for kids™

SMART SEX STUFF FOR KIDS™ PRODUCTS
available at
www.smartsexstuffforkids.com

💜 **SMART SEX STUFF FOR KIDS: A Book of Practical Information & Ideas for Kids 7-17 & Their Parents & Teachers**/Straight Stuff/Girl Stuff/ Boy Stuff/Hot Stuff/Serious Stuff & Smart Stuff+ the latest facts on AIDS/Illustrated/Glossary/Index

💜 **SMART SEX STUFF WORKBOOK**/ Reproducible worksheets for use with all books

💜 **Carole Marsh USER'S GUIDE TO SMART SEX STUFF FOR KIDS™ Books**/Excellent resource

💜 **"Like a Virgin": HOW TO CONVINCE KIDS TO ABSTAIN FROM SEX**

💜 **COULD YOUR KIDS "DIE LAUGHING?": AIDS & TODAY'S KIDS**

💜 **HOW TO GET KIDS OUT OF SCHOOL WITHOUT AIDS, A DISEASE, OR A BABY!**

💜 **(FIRST) AIDS: FRANK FACTS FOR KIDS** In plain English for all ages

155

💜 **A PERIOD IS MORE THAN A PUNCTUATION MARK**/Especially for girls

💜 **SPERM, SQUIRM & OTHER SQUIGGLY STUFF**/Especially for boys

💜 **AIDS-ZITS: A 'SEXTIONARY' FOR KIDS 7-17**/Excellent resource

💜 **MY LIFETIME OF SEX & HOW TO HANDLE IT**/Puts it all in perspective

💜 **"ABSTINENCE" MAKES THE HEART GROW FONDER**/You can convince kids

💜 **"I CON. . . IF YOU CONDOM": THE INS & OUTS OF CONTRACEPTION**

💜 **THE TRUTH (& CONSEQUENCES) OF SEXUALLY TRANSMITTED DISEASES**

💜 **YOU CHOOSE THE ENDING!**/Fictional sex situations & alternative actions & consequences; Brings facts of life "to life" + good test of child's understanding/all ages

💜 **SEX (DRIVER'S) ED**/Multiple-choice quiz on how to survive sexually+score meaning

💙 **(SEX) LIFE ISN'T FAIR!**/Sex, dating, etc. related Murphy's Laws for Kids/Humor

💙 **THE BABY GAME**/Any number can play-is not a board game/Each player has a baby and "cards" give instructions on what to do for it. Very humorous + points out consequences of parenthood!

💙 **"NINE MONTHS IN MY MOMMY": AN AUTOBIOGRAPHY**/Fictional first-person autobiography gives kids respect for unborn child/KIDS WILL NEVER TAKE LIFE LIGHTLY AGAIN!

💙 **"Hello In There!": POETRY TO READ TO THE UNBORN BABY**/EXCELLENT!

Help us help kids be sex safe & sex smart!
Thank you!

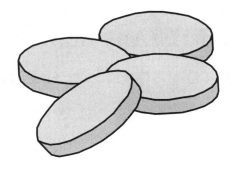

Too Young?

Maine took a proactive step in offering middle school students birth control. This caused a flurry of media attention, as many argued if this was an appropriate step. Some may be surprised to learn that Maine was not the first area to offer these services; Seattle and Baltimore have offered these services for years.

FINALLY!

158